DAYLILIES
FOR THE GARDEN

DAYLILIES
FOR THE GARDEN

Graeme Grosvenor

TIMBER PRESS
Portland, Oregon

Cover 'Christmas Day'
Title page 'Banana Republic'

First published in North America in 1999
by Timber Press Inc.
The Haseltine Building
133 S.W. Second Avenue, Suite 450
Portland, Oregon 97204, U.S.A.

Reprinted 2000

ISBN 0–88192–427–X

A catalog record for this book is available from
The Library of Congress

Designer: Richard Francis
Illustrator: Lesley Boston
Photographer: Graeme Grosvenor

Set in Bembo 11/13
Printed Singapore by Kyodo Printing Co.

10 9 8 7 6 5 4 3 2

Contents

1
Introduction

The hemerocallis, or, as it is more commonly known, the daylily, is an ancient plant from Asia. It probably had its origins in China but there is little doubt that some species have come from other countries in the region. References to the daylily go back over 2000 years. The daylily was certainly known to the Greeks in early Christian times. It is from the Greek words *hemero* meaning 'one day', and *callis* meaning 'beauty', that Linnaeus, in 1753 named the genus *Hemerocallis*.

By the 16th century daylilies were well known in Europe but it was not until the late 19th century that they were introduced into the USA and there is little reference to daylilies in Australia or New Zealand before the mid 20th century.

In a number of ways, the common name for hemerocallis, 'daylily', is an unfortunate one. Firstly, the hemerocallis is not a lily although the flowers do have a resemblance in form to the Asiatic liliums. Secondly, while each individual flower does, or did until recently, last only one day, the typical hemerocallis clump will produce an enormous number of flowers that extends bloom over many weeks. With re-bloom, some cultivars can be in bloom for many months.

Unfortunately, many gardeners are put off by the name and it is not uncommon for some people to even think that daylilies flower for only one day in the year. I can remember a group from a gardening club who visited our display garden at Rainbow Ridge Nursery in Sydney. The garden was ablaze with colour—literally thousands of daylily blooms to enjoy—and one person was telling members of the group, with some air of authority, how lucky they were to have come on *the* one day when so many were in flower.

Opposite 'Moon Twilight'

Another unfortunate misconception about hemerocallis is that they are to be found only in shades of yellow and orange. No doubt this is because of the mass plantings of species hemerocallis that people observe. Without exposure to the great colour range that hybridisers in recent times have given us, these gardeners think only of yellow-orange when thinking about daylilies. Hemerocallis blooms are now available in almost every colour of the rainbow with the single exception being blue. Despite this exception, I think a more suitable common name for the hemerocallis is the 'rainbow lily'.

Up until recently, I think a further barrier to the acceptance of daylilies as one of the outstanding garden perennials has been one of their major attributes—and I refer here to their hardiness. It has always seemed an anomaly to me that we struggle to grow rare, unusual and difficult plants in our gardens when there are so many beautiful plants that are so easy to grow. Daylilies are tough, easy-to-grow plants and their very hardiness has led to them being despised by some, much in the way some gardeners regard the ubiquitous dietes and agapanthus. Landscapers, however, love these latter two plants because of their hardiness and ease of culture.

Landscapers are starting to use daylilies for similar situations and this will continue—particularly when more landscapers, and also landscape architects, discover the huge range of colours and patterns now available. This will flow on to an increased interest from the general public. All that is needed is for these people to be better educated to the absolute beauty and ease of culture of daylilies. Hopefully this book will help in this regard.

There are evergreen and dormant varieties of daylilies and consequently there is a variety suitable for every climatic condition. I must admit to having a love affair with the dormant cultivars but I have observed that the general public has a preference for evergreens. From my own experience as a nurseryman, in areas suited to either type, the evergreens outsell the dormant varieties in a ratio of more than four to one. To me, there is something special about a dormant daylily. It will 'self clean' its foliage as it dies down in the autumn and the new lush foliage in spring is a sight to behold. I find the young foliage in spring just as attractive as that of the wonderful hostas. I can certainly tolerate that bare spot in winter while awaiting the *reverdie* of spring. As the new growth bursts forth in spring I often marvel at the varying shades of green, the variously shaped foliage and the beautiful veining apparent in so many cultivars.

Hybridisers from the USA deserve the highest praise as they have developed the daylily from a rather simple, ordinary plant to one of beauty beyond the realms of the imagination. While there is work being done in developing the daylily in other countries, it is in the USA that the vast bulk of advanced hybridising has been done. Thanks to them, we now have, as well as the original yellows and oranges, a range of beautiful pastel creams, pinks, apricots and blends of these colours. There are also vivid reds, rich purples, subtle mauves and lavenders, and various shades of burgundy, violet, russet, brown and gold. Rich dark reds and purples now approach black. There are pure self colours, blends, bitones, bicolours, polychromes and fancy patterns. Blooms have contrasting or complementary coloured edges and borders. Some are ruffled or have picoteed rims, contrasting eyes, throats and watermark effects. Some have a combination of several of these patterns or features. The 'whites' have become whiter and many are now acceptable as close to pure white. A true blue is still, however, a hybridiser's dream but despite that, there is, I believe, something for every taste.

Clumps of many modern cultivars will carry up to 50 or more flowers on a single scape (flowering stem), will produce numerous scapes over an extended period of time, and then re-bloom at intervals during the year. Also, as the 20th century draws to a close, we now have some varieties of daylilies that flower for two days.

Bloom can be expected to start in very late spring to early summer. This early summer flourish lasts around six weeks or more. Most varieties will re-bloom in autumn and some remain in a state of almost continuous bloom from summer through and into winter. I am not aware of any other perennial that will provide anything like the bloom of an established clump of one of the more floriferous daylily varieties.

My own experience with daylilies has been a long and rewarding one and I am delighted to have seen the wonderful developments that have occurred in recent years. With all the beauty that is now available and the fact that daylilies are suited to a wide range of climatic and soil conditions, I am sure interest in daylilies as garden plants will increase dramatically all over the world in coming years. This growth in interest has started in the USA where daylilies now rank as one of the USA's favourite perennials. No doubt, Australian, New Zealand and European gardeners will develop a similar love affair in time.

Overall, growing daylilies is a fascinating and rewarding hobby. The plants are so easy to grow, relatively free of pests and diseases, and so adaptable that a spot can always be found for them in any garden no matter how congested. They are ideal companion plants for just about anything that can be grown in a sunny or semi-shaded position with reasonable drainage. For productivity they are right at the top of the class and, when this productivity is matched by ease of culture, they justify the tag of 'perfect perennial'.

Daylilies come in dormant or evergreen forms, with flower size ranging from less than 5 cm (2 in) to over 20 cm (8 in), and with flowering height ranging from a very low 20 cm (8 in) to over 2 m (79 in). They also come in a near-complete colour range and a fascinating range of bloom forms. They are ideal in the garden and also a satisfactory cut flower. If, after all this, you don't like them you can eat them. Yes, eat them! Daylilies are an excellent gourmet vegetable and have been used for centuries by the Chinese in their cooking. All parts of the daylily are edible, so it offers the final bonus of being, by far, the most attractive vegetable in the garden or, alternatively, the most practical of flowing ornamentals.

2
The daylily plant

A daylily plant

Daylilies are fibrous-rooted, herbaceous perennials. The roots are elongated and finger-like, varying from thin and thread-like to large, elongated, fleshy and tuberous. The point where the roots meet the fans of foliage is called the crown and it is from the crown that the scapes, or flowering stems that carry the blooms, emerge. It is also from the crown that the plant increases to form a clump over time. The increases are called ramets.

The rate at which a plant increases will vary from cultivar to cultivar. Most are very quick to increase but a very few are frustratingly slow. This rate of increase will determine the frequency with which a clump will need to be divided. However, all cultivars can be left in the ground a minimum of three years without the need for lifting and dividing. Many can be left a lot longer without any deterioration in quality or quantity of bloom. The plant increases in a radial pattern that results in a mound of foliage that is very attractive in itself. In full growth, the daylily plant will have a mass of rich green orchid-like foliage rising anything from 15 cm (6 in) to over 1 m (39 in) in height.

From very late spring to early summer, flowering scapes will rise above the foliage and carry buds to provide a succession of blooms. It is considered a major fault if the scapes do not rise well above the foliage as this results in the flowers opening among the leaves and therefore obscuring them in part or fully.

Depending on variety, scapes will vary in height, number of branches and the number of buds that they carry. Ideally, the height of scape and height of the mound of foliage should be balanced to give a pleasing overall effect. Good branching enables the flowers to be well displayed and high bud count ensures a long season of bloom and a strong visual impact. As a rough rule I think a good scape should carry 20 to 30 blooms. A minimum is ten buds. A stem with more than 50 can become cluttered.

The typical daylily flower is lilium-like in appearance. The flower has six petals in two sets of three. Often the outer three petals are referred to as sepals and only the inner three called petals. The sepals and petals are offset one to the other so it gives the appearance that the petals overlap the sepals to give a fuller and larger outline. Size of flower and width of floral parts will vary considerably both within the species and the hybrids.

Emerging from the throat of the flower are the stamens and a single long style with a stigmatic lip (divided into three parts) held well above the stamens. There are usually six stamens with pollen-bearing anthers at the ends of filaments usually slightly more than half the length of the style.

Kwanzo (a form of *Hemerocallis fulva*)

'Tropical Centrepiece'

'Woodside Ruby'

'Mokan Butterfly'

'Fiesta Fling'

'Royal Prestige'

'Iowa Greenery'

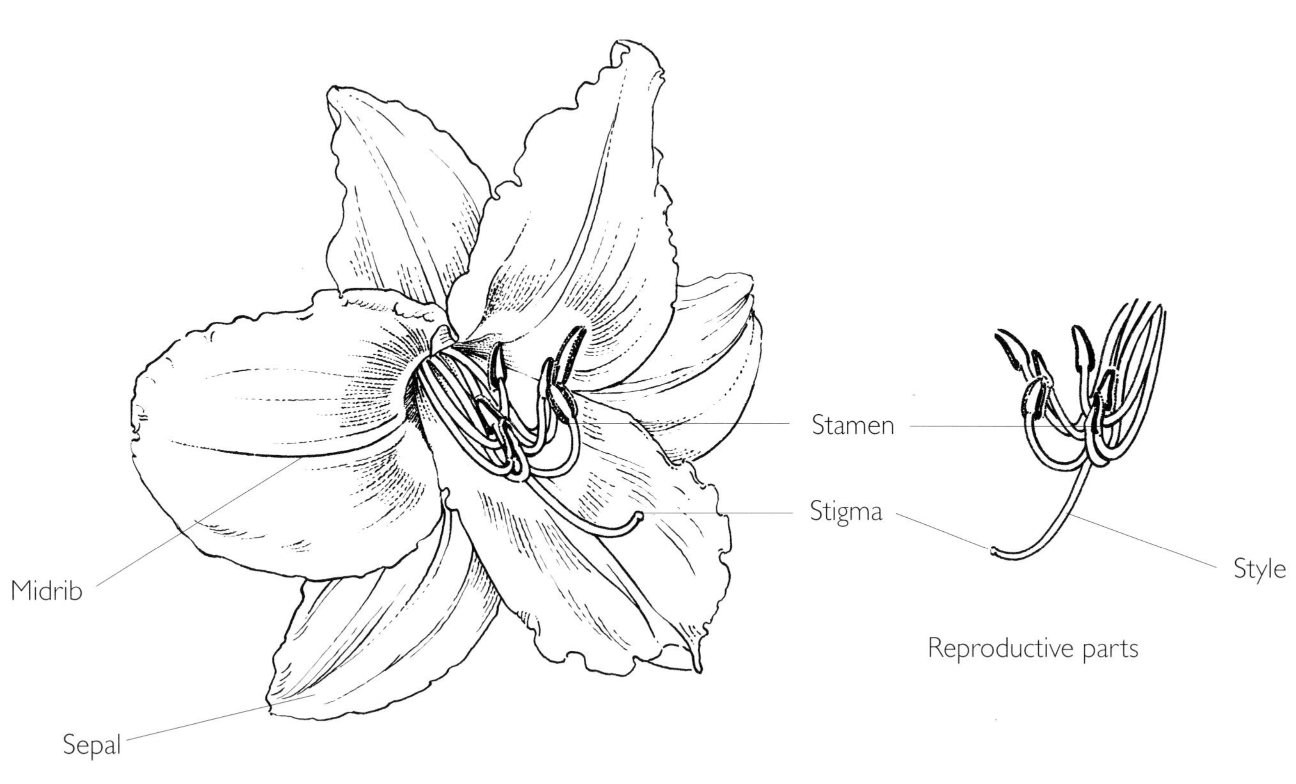

A daylily flower

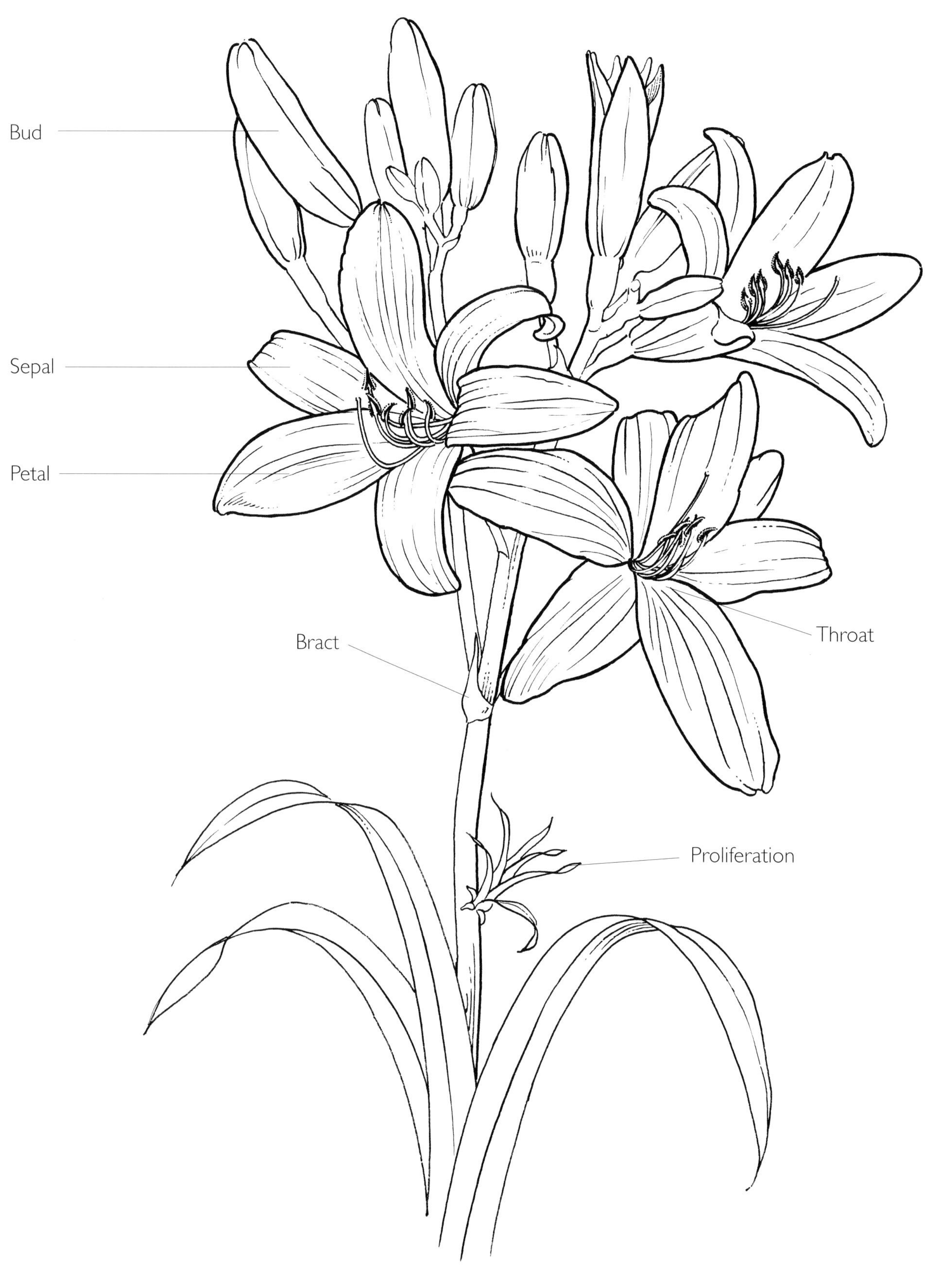

A daylily scape

The Species

Dr A.B. Stout's book on daylilies, published in 1934, was the first major work to systematically classify the various hemerocallis species. Although there have been updates and additions since then, Stout's book still gives the best insight into the species and early hybrids. There will be no attempt in this book to repeat much of or enlarge upon what is in Stout's book. I wish only to make mention of a few of the more significant species that those gardeners who have an interest in the origins of a plant may find of interest.

Hemerocallis fulva is a vigorous plant with light green, coarse foliage that reaches 90 cm (35 in) in height. Flowering scapes reach 1.3 m (51 in) in height and carry up to 20 flowers. Colour is a tawny orange with some variation. Flowers are reasonably full but thinly textured. They, however, hold from dawn to dusk. There is a double flowered form, often referred to as 'kwanzo'. This species daylily is commonly grown. *Photo p. 10*

***Hemerocallis lilioasphodelus* (*H. flava*)** is also very commonly grown and is the daylily best known by non-daylily people. Foliage reaches 90 cm (35 in) in height and is dark green in colour. Flowering scapes reach 1.1 m (43 in) with up to 15 or more flowers in clear lemon yellow. The blooms are full and wide and long lasting, often retaining some colour into the second day.

Hemerocallis citrina has dark green foliage reaching up to 1 m (39 in) in height. Flowering scapes are multi-branched, carry 40 and at times even more than 50 flowers and reach 1.2 m (47 in) in height. The flowers are large, with long and narrow petals. Bloom is nocturnal with flowers opening at or about dusk and blooming through to mid morning. Colour is pale yellow.

Hemerocallis aurantiaca is known as the 'orange fulva daylily'. It grows slightly shorter than *H. fulva*, has shorter scapes, darker green foliage and a less full flower. Basic colour is orange, often tinged with red.

Hemerocallis thunbergii is a late-flowering species of good garden value. It grows to 0.9 m (36 in) with dark green foliage and tall scapes to 1.2 m (47 in) carrying many lemon-yellow flowers on well-branched scapes. It is floriferous and vigorous.

Hemerocallis multiflora reaches 0.5 m (20 in) in height with fine foliage and thin scapes well branched and carrying many chrome yellow flowers over an extended period. Flowering scapes reach 0.7 m (28 in) in height.

Hemerocallis nana reaches 0.35 m (12 in) in height with mid green foliage and scapes that carry from one to three flowers in an orange colour. It is of interest because of its low growth habit.

Other species listed by Dr Stout that I will not touch on are:

Hemerocallis dumortier
Hemerocallis exaltata
Hemerocallis forrestii
Hemerocallis longituba
Hemerocallis middendorffii
Hemerocallis minor
Hemerocallis plicata

In 1968, Dr Shiu-Ying Hu listed several additional species to those recorded above. These include:

Hemerocallis altissima
Hemerocallis coreana
Hemerocallis esculenta
Hemerocallis graminea
Hemerocallis harunensis
Hemerocallis littorea
Hemerocallis micrantha
Hemerocallis pedicellata

Some other recorded species are:

Hemerocallis darrowiana
Hemerocallis yezoensis

While in no way decrying the interest that can be evoked in the growing and studying of various species, I have little doubt that the majority of gardeners will find significantly more interest in the huge range of hybrids now available. So much has been achieved in the last 30 years and so much more is promised in the foreseeable future.

3
Cultivation

The number of people who love their gardens, plants and flowers but who are always trying to grow plants unsuitable for their climate never ceases to amaze me. So many gardeners are attracted by the challenge of doing something that others cannot do, or they just have a desire to overcome adversity. I am sure that many valuable and beautiful plants meet an untimely end in the vain attempts of their owners to do the impossible.

There are no such challenges with daylilies!

Major factors influencing the type of daylily to grow

Daylilies are among the hardiest of plants and there are varieties suitable for any climate and almost any position in a garden. In deciding which varieties to grow for your particular situation you should consider two factors.

Climate

Daylilies will flourish in very cold and very hot climates and in everything in between. Obviously, dormant varieties are at their best in cold climates (such as the northern states of the USA, the most southerly part of Tasmania in Australia, the South Island of New Zealand and the northern parts of Europe), while the evergreen cultivars are at their best in hot, tropical climates (such as the southern states of the USA, the northern part of Australia, and parts of Asia).

In areas with more temperate climatic conditions, both dormant and evergreen daylilies will perform well. There is also an abundance of semi-evergreen cultivars which will perform quite well over the full climatic range. Sometimes a bit of trial and error is required to determine if a variety will do well in a particular climate. But usually you will be able to get good advice on the suitability of a variety for a particular climate from other growers or nurseries.

I am very fortunate in that my nursery and display garden, Rainbow Ridge, is located in a region of Australia with a temperate climate. The hilly area some 30 kilometres west of Sydney (latitude around 33°S) is suited to all types of daylilies. It is never too cold in winter for the evergreens, but it is sufficiently cold for the dormant cultivars. It is important to remember that in deciding which daylily varieties to grow, the most important aspect of climatic conditions is winter cold rather than summer heat. Daylilies, even dormant varieties, revel in the heat of summer!

Position

Daylilies will grow in dry, well-drained or even wet boggy positions. Daylilies are not even particular about soil type or pH. Daylilies will survive the vagaries of the weather including occasional droughts and floods. They are tolerant even of snow, frost, high winds, and

Opposite 'David Kirchoff'

salt spray. They grow well in mountainous country, in flat coastal areas or in inland regions. They will grow in sun or part shade (but as discussed further below) they need some sun to flower well.

For optimum performance, especially quantity of bloom, I believe daylilies require a fair amount of sunlight but they do not necessarily require full sun. They are tolerant of semi-shade but the number of flowers will decrease as the shade increases. I have grown some of the nicest of flowers in semi-shaded positions and feel quite confident that as long as the plants are given either several hours of direct sunshine or a full day in dappled sunshine, performance will be good.

Daylilies are great competitors when used with other plants and, in most cases, where competition for space and nutriment is a concern the daylily will perform well.

It is recommended, however, that for optimum performance, they should not be planted so that they have to compete with the roots of large trees or in a position where they are heavily shaded by or likely to be overgrown by trees or shrubs. When planting daylilies in association with trees it is a good rule of thumb to plant your daylilies at or beyond the perimeter of the canopy.

Some particular daylily cultivars may also require slightly different conditions than others for optimum performance. Some require full sun to bring out their best colour and absolutely revel in the hottest of summer days while others will 'bleach' and 'grease' in the hottest sun but be most beautiful in a semi-shaded position. Again, experiences of other growers or nurseries, and trial and error, will determine perfect positioning but a good guide is that the paler colours will usually accept the most sun while the darker reds and purples are less tolerant and perform best when given some protection from the hot afternoon sun. Hybridisers have worked hard on sun-fastness and most of the more recent releases have much improved substance and are very well equipped to handle all but the hottest of hot days. One of the great joys of growing daylilies is the fact that the flowers last only one day and when other plants can be devastated by extreme heat the daylily is back to its very best as soon as a hot day or hot spell is over.

Ground preparation

While drainage and soil preparation are not as critical for daylilies as they are for many other plants you get the best results if you give your daylilies a well-prepared position with good drainage. Daylilies will grow well in heavy loam to light sandy soils. They perform well in acid or slightly alkaline soils and a pH range between 6 and 8 will give good results.

Soil should be worked to a depth of 15 cm to 30 cm (6 in to 12 in) to create a friable medium. Soil can be improved by the incorporation of compost, well rotted manure or any of the soil conditioners now available. Fertility can be improved by the addition of superphosphate, blood and bone or a complete fertiliser with an N:P:K rating close to 5:10:10.

Daylilies do like to be well watered regularly. They will repay you handsomely for your care and consideration.

Planting time

Daylilies can be planted throughout the year in all but the coldest climates but I have found that autumn and early spring are ideal times for establishing new plants. Plants set out in early to mid autumn establish quickly as there is still sufficient warmth in the soil to promote new root growth. By getting the plants well entrenched before winter cold sets in, they come away more quickly in spring which means that the quality of bloom in the first flowering season after planting is so much the better.

When the soil starts to warm in late winter/early spring we come into another excellent planting time as plants establish very quickly in spring when the days lengthen and temperatures rise. With good after-care, daylilies planted in early spring will still bloom in late spring or early summer although such bloom may not reach the same quality as that from well established clumps.

Except for those areas with extremely cold winters, there is no reason to avoid planting in winter if this suits. Plants will take longer to establish but will perform no worse than those planted in early spring. Daylilies can also be planted in summer, but care needs to be taken to ensure that they are well watered until actively growing again.

'Shaolin Priest'

'Siloam Double Classic'

Right 'Shinto Etching'

How to plant

In general, plants from commercial suppliers will consist of one or two fans of foliage attached to a crown from which also emerge some roots. The foliage and roots will most likely have been trimmed back. Plant by digging a hole and making a small mound in the middle. Place the crown of the plant on the mound and carefully spread the roots evenly down the sides of the mound. I like to add a small quantity, say a teaspoonful, of 8–9 month slow release fertiliser around the roots at planting time. Care should be taken to ensure that the crown is not less than 2.5 cm (1 in) or more than 5 cm (2 in) below what will be the surface of the soil. Planting too deeply will result in lack of bloom and poor increase. Once the crown is covered with soil, the surface of the soil can be dished inward a little to ensure water is captured and directed to the roots. Plants should be firmed in solidly and well watered until the foliage is re-established.

Plants purchased from nurseries and delivered through the mail have a habit of being delayed in the mail, or sent during the hottest periods, or arriving at the most inconvenient of times. If newly arrived plants arrive dry or otherwise stressed or if you will not be able to plant for some time then they should be soaked in water overnight. Only the roots and crown need to be immersed in water.

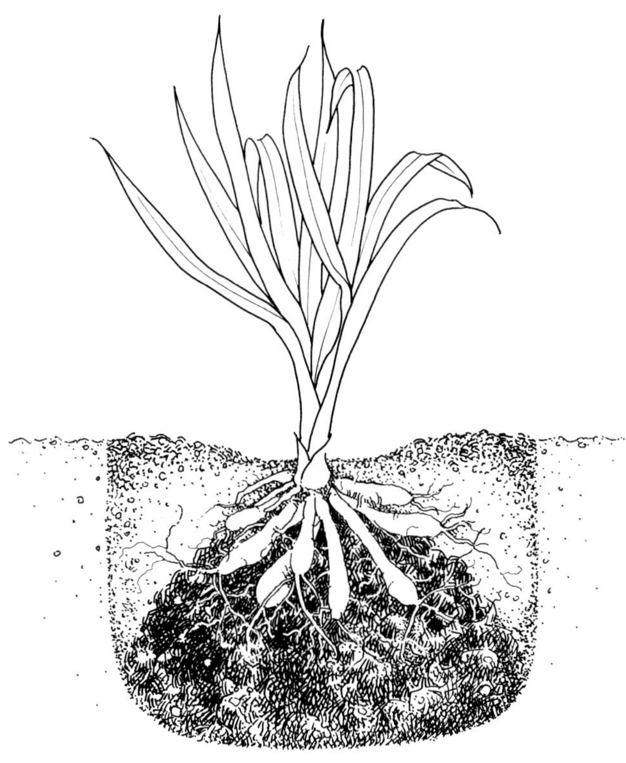

Planting a daylily

If you do not have the ground ready for planting when plants arrive and you will not be ready for a week or more, then it is advisable to heel them in temporarily by digging a shallow trench in a shady position and covering the roots with a light sandy soil which should be kept moist. This will ensure the plants are still in top condition when you are ready to plant.

When dividing a clump and replanting the divisions in your own garden or when giving or receiving a division from a friend, the gardener is in control of the size of the divisions and of the time of moving. The latter is important as you can avoid adverse weather conditions especially extremely hot days. There is no maximum size for a division, but generally, it will consist of one to four fans. The larger the division, the quicker the impact of bloom.

Spacing and positioning of your daylilies is really a question of personal taste and how big the division is that you are planting. You may want a massed planting, or alternatively, you may want to highlight a smaller number of varieties by growing each as a specimen amongst other garden plants. Much has also been said and written in recent times about colour co-ordination. I am much in favour of beautiful pictures being 'painted' in the garden with flowering plants. However, the positioning of different colours and patterns in a mass planting should be done to give you, the gardener, pleasure. I am often asked to give advice on these issues and, while always trying to be helpful, I am adamant that you, the gardener, should do what pleases you most. After all it is your garden. No one can tell you what you like and any advice I give is always prefaced by this statement.

Most daylilies are robust growers and quick increasers and as a general rule it is advisable to leave at least 60 cm–70 cm (more than 2 ft) between plants to allow for future growth. For those gardeners who like a massed effect the 60 cm–70 cm spacing will give this effect in a couple of seasons. Closer planting is possible if an immediate mass effect is wanted. For those who like to see established clumps grown for the beauty of the individual clump and planting, I believe that a distance of at least 90 cm (3 ft) is required from other plants to give this effect unless clumps are going to be dug and replanted quite often. These are all suggestions for large-flowered daylilies. If you are planting miniatures or some small-flowered varieties these distances can be halved in most cases. There are some special cases, particularly among the small-flowered varieties, where the small flowers are developed on large vigorous plants and these should be planted according to the suggestions for large-flowered cultivars.

Labels

To label or not to label, that is the question! If you decide to label, how to label is an even more difficult question. This is not really an issue of cultivation, but if and how plants are labelled can have a major impact on the appearance of a daylily clump and on the appearance of the garden as a whole.

Some gardeners have the rare ability to enjoy their plants without having to know the names of their plants, and do not want labels messing up their beautiful garden. Others are more demanding and structured in their approach, which makes knowing the names of plants essential. I personally like to be able to read and hear about how the varieties I am growing perform for others and I like to be able to tell visitors to the garden the names of plants so they too can acquire them from nurseries. So I must have my precious plants labelled.

While plans of gardens can be created and annotated with names, these can get out of date and lost and so for me they are, at best, a back-up. However, I know of some commercial growers who do not label any of the plants in their gardens and rely completely on a planting guide. Under this system, there are major problems that have to be overcome when plants are being moved around.

How best to label? I confess that I have tried many systems and am yet to find a perfect solution. Just where the compromise between clear and legible labelling and obtrusive interference with the beauty of the plant exists I leave to the judgment of the gardener.

I currently use old venetian blinds cut to 25 cm (10 in) lengths as the base and write on them with an Artline 400 XF paint marker pen for most stock plantings. I have in the past used Dymo labels adhered to venetian blinds and also hand writing on venetian blinds using a soft (6B) pencil.

Specimen labelling in the nursery is difficult as labels need to be large and clear and so can easily become obtrusive. Large plastic push-in labels with a rectangular writing area are ideal for customer recognition and writing on such labels using the Artline 400 will provide a minimum of two seasons' clear labelling. Aesthetically this leaves me cold as the nursery becomes a garden of labels. At this stage, I have no better solution. In the home garden, where you have only yourself to satisfy, the labelling can be much less obtrusive. For example, labels can be positioned at the back of plants.

After-care

Once your daylily is planted there is a degree of care and attention needed to obtain optimum results.

Watering

Control of water is essential to all gardening and this is no less the case with growing daylilies even though they are drought-resistant and will survive with only a small amount of natural rainfall. Daylilies benefit from heavy watering two to three times a week during spring and summer. This will ensure quantity and quality of bloom and maximum re-bloom. How heavy the watering should be is a function of heat and wind, and hence evaporation, and underlying soil moisture level. Plants should not be watered to such an extent that the soil becomes boggy or nutriment is leached from it.

I find watering in the evening when there is less evaporation or very early in the morning most beneficial. Watering during the day is less effective and overhead watering when blooms are open should be avoided if possible to ensure that flowers do not become spotted or marked. Modern irrigation techniques and equipment have made life much easier and should be used if possible. The use of electro/mechanical timers, polypipe, high quality dripline and micro-sprayers is highly recommended for daylily culture.

Mulching

Given the importance of water, water retention around your plant is very important to maximise the benefit of the watering and to minimise waste. To this end mulching is important and I like to see daylilies heavily mulched once they are established. There are many very suitable mulches but availability and cost are major factors. Well-rotted animal manures and/or garden compost are excellent. Purchased mulches and soil conditioners such as mushroom compost, various barks and wood chips or shavings, and lucerne hay have great merit.

Fortunately, daylilies are not 'finicky' or difficult plants that require the pH of such mulches to be within precise bounds so the most important issue for best results is to provide a mulch. I suppose it is possible to provide too much mulch but I must confess to having put it on in very thick layers at times with nothing but beneficial results.

Mulching has the added benefit of helping with weed control. Mulching reduces the number of weeds as well as making it easier to weed. Unfortunately, it does not eliminate weeding altogether. It also ensures the addition of some nutriment to the soil and can provide a most attractive surrounding to the plant.

Weed control

Weed control is essential for any garden planting to be healthy, vigorous and attractive and if one has mulched well and has the time and energy, and a back which has not given in to time and wear, then occasional hand weeding can even be relaxing and enjoyable. Most gardeners will, however, look elsewhere for weed control.

Other approaches can involve the use of weedmat or thickly laid newspaper covered with pebbles, stones, scoria, gravel or other ornamental covers. The use of certain chemicals that inhibit weed germination can work well with daylilies. Trifluran in its various commercial forms and namings (e.g. Treflan and Surflan) is a satisfactory chemical which will inhibit the germination of many weeds without any ill effects to the daylilies. It works well against most annual grasses and many broad-leafed weeds but has no effect on others such as clover. Before using any of these types of chemicals you should seek advice from the manufacturer on their use with daylilies and from other growers on their success with such products.

Once weeds have germinated there are many chemical knock-down or systemic sprays to kill them but extreme care must be taken as they can have a similar kill effect on daylilies. An example of a knock-down spray is Tryquat. Glyphosate forms the base of a number of well-known systemic sprays such as Roundup and Zero.

Selective herbicides are not common but Fusilade will kill some newly germinated annual grasses that get in among daylily plantings and, if used in accordance with the maker's instructions will have no ill effect on the daylilies. But, as mentioned above seek advice before using these products.

'Glazed Heather Plum'

'Green Dragon'

'Jedi Dot Pierce'

'Gentle Shepherd'

'Grapes of Wrath'

'Study in Scarlet'

'Ever So Ruffled'

Fertilising

Of course the provision of food as well as water is part of after-care but it is a very special part. It never ceases to amaze me that customers will spend large sums of money on quality plants and will then neglect them, allowing them to struggle rather than flourish. I have often used the approach that just as humans and other animals need food and water, so also do plants. People usually understand.

Once again I must stress that daylilies are easy care and will survive without a regular fertilising program. However, this virtue can lead to their neglect. Optimum results can only be obtained by providing optimum conditions, including a balanced diet. Haphazard fertilising is probably better than none at all but a well-organised program is desirable. Over fertilising can be a problem particularly at planting time or if too much nitrogen is provided. The latter can result in an abundance of lush foliage and a corresponding decrease in the quantity and quality of flowers. Too much nitrogen often leads to long leggy scapes with small flowers. Care should also be taken when fertilising newly planted daylilies. In fact my preference is to use only slow release fertilisers with young plants until they have been in the ground for at least six months so as to avoid burning new roots.

Phosphorus is essential to plants coming into flower, particularly if seeds are going to be set. Adequate supplies of phosphorus will help to provide good quality flowers and the best and cheapest source of phosphorus is superphosphate. Potash is essential for plants to make up a strong, efficient root system and produce good plant increase. It is best supplied as potassium sulphate.

Many of the mulches already mentioned will provide suitable fertilising material. This is particularly true of animal manures and lucerne hay. The use of a slow release fertiliser at planting time has already been mentioned and is a very satisfactory means of supplying nutriment to a plant in small doses over an extended period of time. Chemical fertilisers with low nitrogen content are beneficial. Any complete rose fertiliser will suffice.

It should be realised that each garden is different in its soil composition and requirements, and consequently, gardeners should develop their own practices. There is an old adage 'if it ain't broke, don't fix it'. If your soil is in good tilth and you grow other plants well then you don't need to do anything other than what you have already been doing and you will grow good daylilies. If you don't grow other plants to your satisfaction, then perhaps daylilies are your answer because they are a lazy gardener's dream.

One last point on feeding is when to fertilise. It is best not to fertilise when plants are coming into bloom as you could induce leaf growth at the expense of flowers. Ideal times are immediately the plants start active growth in late winter–early spring, immediately after the first flourish, and then, according to variety, immediately after subsequent flushes of bloom.

Dividing and replanting

Well now, you have selected the plants suitable for your climate, you have found an ideal position, you have prepared your ground well, planted correctly and given all the proper after-care. You have enjoyed beautiful bloom and copious re-bloom for three or more years. It is now time to move on and this moving on can take various forms but the most common form is to lift and divide your daylily and then replant. I have used three years as a starting point but this is by no means definitive nor even a realistic suggestion. There is little doubt that daylilies can be left in the ground for several more years very often with little, if any, deterioration in bloom. Much will depend on the vigour of your plant and your cultivation. Invariably, if you have left your plant too long without dividing, it will tell you that you need to get to work by giving inadequate performance. Hopefully things won't be left that long.

The timing to lift and divide is not critical, but note earlier comments. A lot depends on:

- the cultivar and its bloom periods;
- the local climate;
- the availability of time and well-prepared ground.

I have found the best times to lift and divide are mid–late autumn followed by late winter/early spring. These are times when there is little or no bloom and any bloom that is around can probably be sacrificed at no great cost. In hot tropical climates I would think that any time through late winter to early spring would be ideal, while in cold climates I would think that early to mid autumn or early to mid spring would be best. Again it is a decision for the gardener to make and once a pattern that is satisfactory is established then it is wise to stay with it.

Lifting a clump

Cutting a division

Planting divisions

A single division (left) and a double division (right)

Those growers who have sufficient space and wish to always have at least one well-established clump of each variety can achieve this by cutting a reasonably large two–three fan division off an established clump in its second or third season and establishing a new clump. When the time comes to lift and divide the original clump there is already another clump well established.

There is some argument about the quality of flowers and scapes on newly planted or divided daylilies as opposed to two-year, three-year and so on clumps. At least one well-known American grower recommends dividing every year and insists that flowers on first year plants are larger and better. It is my experience that this is true of some very vigorous cultivars and the autumn bloom on many newly planted varieties is superb but, in general, I believe the best flowers and the best scapes are on second and third year clumps.

Established clumps have their roots very well set into the ground and they should be gradually loosened with a heavy garden fork by working around the clump until it is free. A fork is usually much superior to a spade for digging daylilies as its use will result in less damage to the roots. Once lifted from the ground the clump can easily be freed from soil by hosing and is then ready for division. A strong sharp carving knife is excellent for this operation. (I suggest you buy one for the garden rather than take one from the kitchen!) I like to cut the clump initially into three or four smaller clumps and then proceed to work on the smaller clumps which can often be divided by hand or cut into plants with two, three or four fans. I prefer to plant multi-fan divisions if possible as they seem to re-establish quicker. When dispatching plants from Rainbow Ridge Nursery we always try to send a double division when stock allows to ensure the customer gets a good start. I know that many nurseries send only single divisions and in my experience these plants will take considerably longer to establish.

If you are replanting in the same position remember to rejuvenate the soil by the addition of compost, soil conditioner, manure and/or fertiliser to ensure the replanted divisions are given every opportunity to flourish.

Many people cannot bear to dispose of healthy plants from their garden and I am one of these. If a daylily continues to give pleasure then it should be replanted and grown while ever it is satisfying. Fortunately, or unfortunately, there are many new daylilies coming on to the market each year and once a plant has been superseded there is a strong argument to replace it. I know that I grow only a very few daylilies that I was growing 20 years or even 10 years ago as so many superior cultivars have reached us in recent years. I am continually updating my collection. I also have the advantage of being able to control stock through the nursery and can decide on which plants should be replanted each season and which ones can be sold right out. It is a tribute to those older daylilies that are still listed in our nursery catalogue that they can hold a place when so many wonderful new cultivars keep becoming available. These older daylilies have been lifted, divided and replanted many times and will continue to be so treated while ever they prove satisfying.

Bloom period

Bloom can be expected to start in very late spring to early summer. This early summer flourish lasts around one to one and a half months. Most varieties will re-bloom in autumn and some remain almost in a state of continuous bloom from summer through and into winter. I am not aware of any other perennial that will provide anything like the bloom of an established clump of a continuous blooming daylily.

4
Propagation

Daylilies can be propagated by division, by proliferation, from seed and by tissue culture.

Division

The main method of propagating daylilies is by division and this has been referred to already on a number of occasions. In essence, part of a clump, usually one, two or three plants, is cut from a parent clump and replanted. These divisions will remain true to all the characteristics of the parent plant.

Physical division is the main method used by commercial growers to propagate daylilies. Propagation by division has been discussed in Chapter 3 and can basically be performed at any time of the year. The more often that parent plants are divided and replanted the quicker the multiplication. That is, a plant which is regularly divided and replanted will produce more plants at the end of, say, a four-year period, than one which is left in the same position and nature allowed to take its course. This is why most nurseries like to lift and divide more often than is recommended for home gardens. The trade-off is more plants rather than spectacular displays of bloom.

Opposite 'Flower Pavilion'

Proliferation

Some daylilies will produce small plants from the axils of flowering scapes. These small plants are called proliferations and, if removed when reasonably mature and planted, will grow true to the parent plant. To produce plants from proliferations you cut the scape about 2 cm (1 in) below the base of the proliferation and establish its roots either by planting directly in the ground or in a mixture of sand and garden soil up to the base of the foliage. Roots are formed very quickly and proliferations will often bloom in the following season. For me, optimum results are achieved by allowing the proliferations to develop on the flowering scape until bloom has finished and roots are already starting to form. This ensures nearly 100% success in propagation. Proliferations are quite common on some cultivars but are never seen on others. They occur more readily on diploid cultivars although I have seen them on tetraploids.

A proliferation on a stem (left) and a planted proliferation (right)

Seed

Seed pod recently set

Mature seed pods

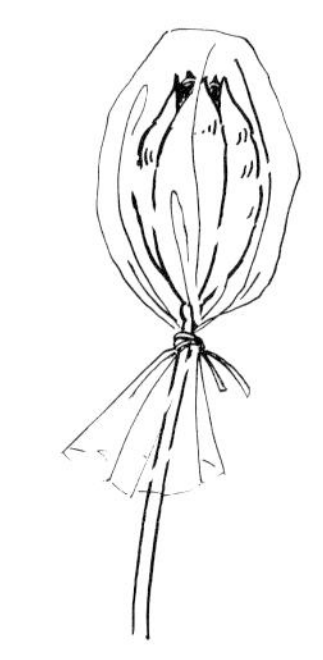

A covered seed pod

Daylilies can be propagated from seed which is the result of either deliberately set crosses or from pods set naturally without human interference. Raising daylilies from seed is a fascinating and rewarding pastime although the rewards in most cases will be emotional rather than financial. New cultivars are developed this way and plants raised from seed will not be true to the 'pod' or 'pollen' parent plants (except in the case of a self cross of a species) although many look-alikes will be obtained. Unfortunately, many seedling plants are inferior to the parents from which they were harvested. Planned crosses, where the pollen from one parent plant is deliberately used to cross-pollinate another plant, have a far greater chance of producing seedlings of merit. This will be discussed more thoroughly in the chapter on hybridising (see Chapter 11).

Successful cross-pollination, whether it be humanly induced or otherwise, will be observed a few days after the flower has bloomed. The ovary at the base of the flower swells. Sometimes the ovary swells but then dries up and drops off. However, within a week it should be obvious if a seed pod has been set. Over the next four to six weeks this seed pod will grow and maintain its green colour. At some stage it will start to brown off and ultimately start to split. This is the ideal time to harvest the seed. If you wish to collect the seed but do not have the opportunity to observe the pod's development day by day I suggest you cover the seed pod with an old stocking or evolution cloth (a product used as a crop cover) and tie it around the stem a little below the seed pod.

Once harvested the seed is best kept cool and allowed to dry out. There are arguments for planting immediately and, while I feel this could be successful in tropical climates, my own experience has been that storage for a little while is better. Seed from pods set in summer can be planted in autumn.

Plant seeds about 1 cm (½ in) below the surface of a good seed-raising mix in a pot or straight into the ground. Most seeds germinate readily and the young plants can be grown on where they have germinated or lined out from pots when they are 2 cm–3 cm (about 1 in) high. I do not suggest lining out in winter, particularly in cold climates. Depending on climate and growing conditions flowers can often be seen in the second season after setting the pod.

Tissue culture

Daylily plants can be propagated by cloning in laboratories. The growth points of a parent plant are divided into a number of very small sections and, after going through a sterilising process to ensure cleanliness, the small sections are developed in a chemical growing medium into small plantlets. These plantlets can be divided again using the same technique. Ultimately, the small plantlets are transferred to a rooting medium and finally into tubes with a potting mix where they are hardened off and then grown on as a nursery plant. Tissue-cultured plants should be true to the original plant and in most cases are. Aberrations sometimes do occur and 'sports' which develop may have very desirable characteristics.

The use of tissue culture is of benefit to nurseries which wish to produce large quantities of plants quickly. It is of little interest to the home gardener and most commercial growers as a means of propagation. Unfortunately, it has been my experience that those plants which are highly desirable but slow increasers are also the ones least prone to successful tissue culture. Their poor growth habits are maintained in the tissue culture process and they are rarely successful. In contrast, those universal good growers will usually respond very well to tissue culture and you will often be 'over successful'. Once established in culture, daylilies will multiply at a rate of between two and three times every dividing period—usually five to six weeks. Because this is exponential growth one can see that under optimum conditions of trebling every five weeks one will soon have an excess of riches. For example, ten multiplications using a three to one rate of increase will produce 1, 3, 9, 27, 81, 243, 729, 2187, 6561, 19 683, 59 049—that is, nearly 60 000 plants—from one in around one year.

Of course, in practice, it doesn't always work like that; if the rate of increase is only two to one then over the one year period a mere 1000 plants would be produced. These numerical examples are also only true if plants are always being used to multiply and no plants are being rooted out for sale.

Tissue culture has advantages and is a very useful approach for nurserymen with large turnovers who wish to produce large quantities of easy growing daylilies. It does not, however, solve the problem of getting poor growers to increase more quickly.

5
Classification

The classification of daylilies would seem, at first glance, a rather complicated and somewhat daunting project. There are so many characteristics which can be used for classification and, as virtually all of them overlap, the novice grower can be left completely bewildered. Let me try to lead you through this maze by stating what the classification groups are going to be and then going through them.

Daylilies can be classified according to:

- Foliage habit;
- Bloom habit;
- Ploidy;
- Flower size;
- Flower form.
- Substance and texture;
- Flowering time;
- Flower colour;
- Colour patterns.

There will also be minor sub-classifications within each group.

I have avoided doing a classification according to scape height as it is not a reliable or precise criterion; scape height will be determined by so many factors such as climate, position, cultivation and care. However, daylily enthusiasts will want to know if daylilies are tall, medium or short in stature and I will endeavour to give heights, as we grow them, for the recommended cultivars discussed later.

Foliage habit

This classification is based on the degree to which the daylily plants retain their foliage in the colder months of the year. It is a measure of dormancy.

Dormant

A dormant (Dor) plant is completely defoliated in winter. We talk of 'hard dormant' where the plants cannot be seen at all and degrees of dormancy where the tips of the fans can be seen at or about soil level. Dormant daylilies are more suitable for colder climates and hence are recommended for more southerly areas in the southern hemisphere and more northerly areas in the northern hemisphere.

Evergreen

An evergreen (Ev) plant retains its foliage throughout the year and is more suitable for warmer climates. Evergreen daylilies are, therefore, recommended for the more northerly parts of the southern hemisphere and the more southerly parts of the northern hemisphere.

Opposite 'Green Widow'

Semi-evergreen

This classification is for those in-between plants which die down and lose some of their foliage but always retain sufficient greenery for the plant to be seen. This is, by far, the most difficult of the three classifications to pinpoint because the degree of defoliation will vary considerably according to climate. In fact, plants registered as semi-evergreen (S–Ev) can be dormant in cold climates and evergreen in hot climates.

It is difficult to give rulings on which daylilies suit particular climates other than the generalisations given previously. Growers should realise that there are no hard and fast rules and there are many exceptions to the generalisations, mainly on the positive side. Virtually all evergreens are excellent in tropical climates but many dormants grow well also, and virtually all dormants are excellent in colder climates but once again many evergreens perform very well also. The semi-evergreen cultivars are obviously very adaptable and usually perform well in any climatic condition but with varying degrees of dormancy.

Do not be put off by the foliage habit if you fancy a particular daylily but talk about its performance with your specialist nursery or other growers in your area. Failing the availability of advice you may wish to take the initiative, grow the plant and evaluate its performance for yourself. My own experiences have been very positive. In the Hills area about 30 kilometres west of the city of Sydney where winters are cold (with temperatures occasionally below 0°C on winter nights but usually around 2°C–3°C) and summers can be quite hot, we have no trouble growing any daylilies and obtain excellent results with dormant and evergreen cultivars and all the variations in between.

Daylilies can and will acclimatise to conditions with which they are unfamiliar and they will often acclimatise very quickly. However, you should never judge a daylily on its first year performance. First flowering usually produces large flowers in moderate quantities but performance on second and subsequent year plants is more typical and, in general, better.

I have often been asked if evergreen or dormant cultivars are better and, of course, this is a question that one cannot answer for anyone else, but my personal preference is for the dormant cultivars. This is based on two factors—I appreciate that the dormant varieties 'clean themselves up' in the winter and hence are always neat and tidy, and I love the beautiful new foliage as it emerges in spring. On an established clump this foliage can be as attractive as the new foliage on the beautiful hostas. One negative factor is that, in winter, spots need to be marked as to where the dormant daylilies are planted. This is a small price to pay, in my opinion, for the rewards given by dormant cultivars.

This preference is an aesthetic one and not commercially based. In spite of my feelings only one in five daylilies sold through our nursery is dormant so popular opinion outweighs my view many times over and, for commercial reasons, we grow a disproportionate number of evergreen cultivars compared with dormants.

A major factor in the popularity of evergreen cultivars, apart from the fact that most gardeners want to see their plants throughout the year, is that the outstanding daylily developments that have taken place in recent years have been mainly in the evergreen cultivars. Many of the world leaders in the hybridising and release of new cultivars are located in the southern states of the USA. Most of their hybridising efforts have been with evergreens so most of the new fancy colours and extravagantly ruffled and edged forms are evergreen. Improvements in colour, form, growth and plant habits continue with dormant cultivars but not at the same pace.

Bloom habit

This classification is based on when the plants flower in the season and is of assistance to those who wish to co-ordinate a planting so as to have a massed display or a display spread over a period of time. In reality this is less important than it would seem as the daylily is a particularly long-flowering perennial and it is normal to have the early, mid season and late-blooming daylilies in bloom simultaneously, although some would be coming to the end of their initial bloom for the season just as others are starting.

The quantity of bloom is determined by the number of flowering scapes that are produced, how these scapes are spaced in terms of the timing of the bloom, and, the number of buds held on each scape. Classification then is early (E), mid season (M), late (L), with minor variations such as very early (VE) for the first to bloom, and very late (VL) for the last to bloom and combinations such as early to mid season (E–M) denoting that plants bloom early and continue into mid season and mid season to late (M–L) denoting that plants commence blooming in mid season and continue until late in the initial bloom season.

The actual timing of bloom is influenced primarily by local climate and, to a lesser extent, by growing conditions. Daylilies usually commence their bloom sometime in the last month of spring, November in the southern hemisphere and May in the northern hemisphere. Warm climates with particularly mild winters may see good bloom up to a month earlier than colder climates. Peak bloom is usually in the first month of summer.

After a rest following initial bloom many daylilies will have one or more further flourishes of bloom and this characteristic or classification is called re-bloom (Re). There are many factors that will determine the timing and quantity of re-bloom. Climatic conditions, seasonal variations in weather pattern, the position the plant has in the garden and the care that it is given will all have an effect on the quantity and quality of re-bloom but primarily the re-bloom can only be obtained if it is a characteristic of the plant.

In evaluating the desirability of a plant for an extended and even continuous bloom display the gardener must look for those daylilies regarded as true re-bloomers (usually denoted as 'Re' in catalogues). Remember then that there is much variability in the quantity and quality of re-bloom but a strong factor in obtaining maximum bloom is the care given to the plant.

If you want as much bloom as possible over an extended period from your daylilies the factors over which you have control are:

- *Selection*—make sure you purchase daylilies with the Re-bloom (Re) notation;
- *Position*—select the sunniest, best-drained position in your garden;
- *Water*—provide plenty of water in the growing season. If drainage is good it is doubtful if you can supply too much water;
- *Fertiliser*—make sure that you provide a good mulch and then fertilise your plants immediately after each flourish of bloom.

Ploidy

A further classification of daylilies is into the division of *diploid* or *tetraploid*. Just about all daylilies offered for sale are one or the other although triploid daylilies do exist. It is this classification—the distinction between diploid and tetraploid—which gives the average non-specialist gardener the most concern and, in reality, it should give the least. Most growers and many specialists are unable to tell the difference between diploid and tetraploid flowers and/or plants.

A diploid contains the basic number of chromosomes for the species in each cell. The hemerocallis species have 22 chromosomes and this is the basic classification for daylilies. Diploids are usually denoted 'Dip' in catalogues. In some catalogues, it is assumed that daylilies are diploid unless otherwise specified so no classification will mean that the variety is a diploid.

In recent years, experiments with the chemical colchicine have enabled scientific gardeners to double the chromosome count in some plants. The daylily is one of those plants and, by treatment, a new breed of daylilies with 44 chromosomes has been created. These daylilies are called tetraploids (denoted 'Tet') and tetraploid daylilies are often simply called 'tets'.

It is the chromosomes, within the nucleus of the cell, which determine the characteristics of a plant. When two plants are cross-pollinated the seed produced will contain chromosomes from both parents and it is this genetic combination which determines the characteristics of the new plant developed from the seed. The differentiation between diploids and tetraploids is very important to hybridisers as genetically the two types are essentially different and it is most unlikely that any cross-pollination between a diploid and a tetraploid will succeed. In the unlikely event that the cross-pollination is successful, the resultant progeny could be diploid, could be tetraploid or could be triploid, in which case the progeny would most likely be sterile and of no further genetic use.

Anybody who is interested in hybridising their daylilies to produce new varieties would have an immediate interest in this classification as it is usually a firm rule that you only cross diploids with diploids and only cross tetraploids with tetraploids. In performing any cross the chance of the resulting seedlings coming 'true' to either parent is very small and the higher the chromosome count the greater the diversity. Thus, by working with tetraploids, hybridisers have been able to develop a much wider range of colours and patterns. Since the initial use of colchicine in the late 1930s, the daylily has been developed to new heights and this development continues at a frantic pace. It should be noted, however, that many of the world's outstanding hybridisers continue to work with diploids and the hybridising of diploid daylilies has reached such a high standard that the better diploids compare very favourably with the average tetraploids and it is only the very best of tetraploids which are clearly superior plants and flowers. Some lovers of diploids might even challenge me on this.

In general, it is argued that tetraploid plants are potentially stronger, better foliaged and have increased vigour in leaf and scapes than diploids. Flowers are larger, more intense in colour and have improved substance. There is the potential for greater variation in pattern and form. However, as already stated, the top quality diploids are also superb and the classification of diploid or tetraploid is primarily of interest to hybridisers.

The three methods of classification so far discussed all refer to the plant and all are mutually exclusive. To use the abbreviations already used, a plant can be:

- Dor, Ev, or S–Ev in terms of its foliage habit;
- E, M, or L in terms of its bloom timing, plus possibly Re if it re-blooms;
- Dip, or Tet depending on the plant's ploidy.

So any particular variety listed in a catalogue will have a combination of these indicators that can be used to determine some basic characteristics of the variety. Typical classifications then would be—'Scarlet Orbit' (Ev, Tet, E, Re) or 'Rose Emily' (Dor, Dip, M, Re).

Apart from the height of the flowering scape, these indicators tell a prospective buyer most that is required with regard to the plant. Such aspects as vigour, rate of increase, etc. are all functions of after-care. The height of the flowering scape to be expected is difficult to predict as it also depends on cultivation. Hybridisers give a registered height when naming their daylilies. Perhaps it would be better if hybridisers did not try to be too precise but rather just gave a more general indication such as Low, Medium or Tall. I have regularly found great disparity between performance in my garden and the registered height. I have no doubt that this will continue to be the case.

It is the case, however, that daylilies are classified in catalogues by height of scape and the height given in most catalogues is usually measured in inches. (The classification of height is often in inches as the central registry for daylilies is in the USA which has not yet gone metric. Most new varieties are developed in the USA.) The important thing to remember is that when you see reference to the height of a scape you should interpret this only as a guide because of variation in position, climate, growing conditions and season.

The height of scapes also varies during the bloom season. Many cultivars will be taller or shorter on re-bloom than on initial bloom. A typical example is the very popular red daylily 'Apple Tart'. This daylily is registered as 70 cm (28 in) in the USA and usually grows taller here. On re-bloom, which often quickly follows the original bloom, the scapes will reach 120 cm (48 in) and some will reach 150 cm (60 in) or more. This is over twice the registered height and is typical of the bloom on 'Apple Tart' in most years.

In contrast, the short growing 'Ruffled Shawl'—a very attractive pink—is invariably shorter in scape height on re-bloom in my Dural garden.

Flower size

Daylilies can be further classified according to their flowers as distinct from their plant habits. Classification of daylilies according to flower size is a natural way of discriminating as the diameter of the blooms varies from a tiny 2.5 cm (1 in) to over 25 cm (10 in). There are three categories for classification of bloom size.

- *Miniature* where the flowers are less than 7.5 cm (3 in) in diameter.
- *Small-flowered* where the flowers are 7.5 cm (3 in) or more but less than 11 cm (4½ in) in diameter.
- *Large-flowered* where the flowers are 11 cm (4½ in) or more in diameter.

In my view flower size should be in proportion to the height of the foliage and scape but this aspect is not taken into consideration when cultivars are named and registered. I find small flowers on tall scapes somewhat difficult to appreciate and I am even less enthused when small flowers are accompanied by large, thick foliage. Others obviously disagree with me, otherwise plants with such characteristics would not be released.

The larger flowered daylilies do not present a similar problem to me and I can fully appreciate large flowers on tall scapes, medium scapes or short scapes. No matter what size the bloom, it is a major fault if the plant produces bloom scapes so short that flowers open in amongst the foliage.

'Kosciusko'

'Grand Palais'

'White Crinoline'

'Cleda Jones'

'Solano Bull's Eye'

Flower form

Number of petals

The first characteristic under which daylilies are classified for flower form is the number of floral parts. Flowers are said to be single, semi-double or double:

• *Single*—most daylilies have six floral parts and these are called singles;

• *Semi-double*—sometimes blooms have extra petaloids and these are called semi-doubles;

• *Double*—flowers with more than six petals are called double. The double daylilies themselves take different forms with the extra segments appearing as tufts of petals in the middle of the flower or as an extra layer or layers of petals. The extent to which 'double' daylilies are, in fact, double will be seen to vary and there are often anomalies in garden performance.

As discussed earlier the typical single daylily flower consists of six floral parts; the three larger parts set to the front of the flower are called petals while the other three parts, usually smaller and set to the back, are called sepals. In many of the species daylilies the floral parts are narrow. Early hybrids have this same characteristic. Many modern hybrids have been developed to a level where the size of the sepals is comparable with that of the petals and both are now much wider.

Some doubles are always double; others are often single while settling in for the first season after being planted or divided, then fully and continuously double once established; while others again are single early in the season even when established, then double on repeat bloom. I have also observed established clumps where single and double blooms are produced simultaneously. The development of double daylilies has been outstanding in recent years and there are now many spectacular, high quality double flowered daylilies available in a very full colour range.

Flower shape or outline

As well as the quantity of petals the shape or outline of the flower created from these petals is another means of classification, independent of whether the flower is single, semi-double or double. The main shapes or outlines are:

• *Circular (or rounded) form*—is very desirable and pleasing in my view. The flowers have a circular outline, usually with overlapping segments to give a full effect. The segments tend to be short and wide. Modern trends in hybridising have been to produce flowers more and more circular in outline with petals and sepals being developed to be comparable in size with one another.

Circular or rounded form

Triangular form—exists when the segments form the basic outline of two overlapping triangles with vertices offset. The sepals often recurve giving a modified triangular effect.

Triangular form

Star-shaped form—exists when the segments tend to be long and pointed, usually with a considerable space between them, giving the effect of a six pointed star.

Star-shaped form

Spider form—exists when the floral parts are long and narrow. A 'true' spider daylily has segments in which the length is five times (or more) the width but there are many 'spider-form' daylilies on the market which are not 'true spiders'. These daylilies have long, narrow segments with the length less then the mandatory five times the width. In recent years, interest in spider daylilies has increased considerably and there are talented hybridisers working to improve this class.

Spider form

Informal form—is a term used to describe blooms which have no easily defined regular shape. While there are daylilies available that could be called 'informal', it is a very limited class.

Tailoring and ruffling

Another basic classification of flower form which is very much part of modern thinking is whether a flower is tailored or ruffled:

Tailored bloom—is plain, smooth and precise in its appearance. Most of the triangular, star and spider types are tailored in appearance. By contrast, a very modern trend is to develop ruffling of the petal edges, particularly in the rounded cultivars on which it produces a spectacular effect.

Tailored bloom

Ruffled bloom—has edges which are raised, indented and crimped to varying degrees. In recent years ruffled blooms have been the most sought after of all daylilies. These are the flamboyant aristocrats of the daylily world and as ruffling increases one wonders if, and when, it will ever cease to be sought by gardeners and hybridisers alike. Many modern hybrids now have heavy 'pie-crust' edges and often the edges of the petals and sepals are so intertwined that the flower has difficulty in opening properly in all but the hottest of weather. It will be interesting to observe how far this most attractive of characteristics can be taken before there is some adverse reaction from the gardening public. Perhaps the development curve is infinite?

Ruffled bloom

Above 'Enduring Love'

Left 'Chemistry'

'Flames of Fortune'

'Virginia Peck'

'Chinese New Year'

'Wedding Band'

'Happy Hooligan'

'High Priestess'

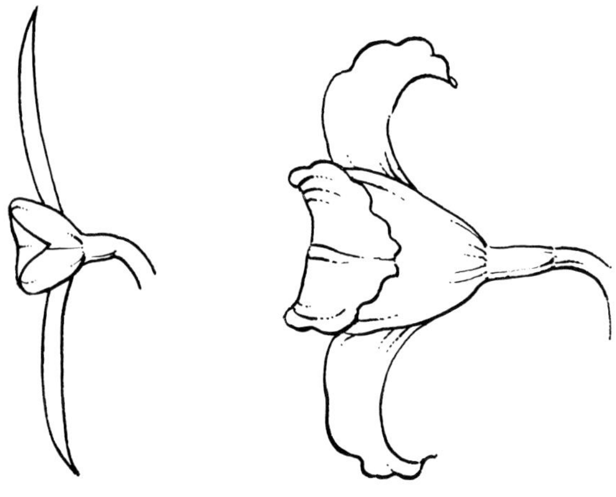

Flat form   Flaring form

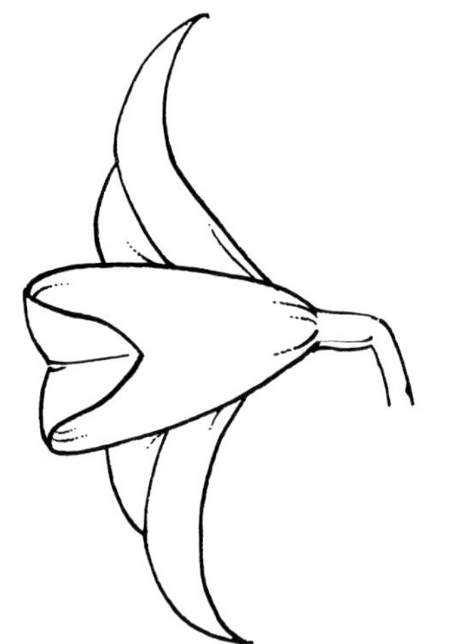

Recurved form

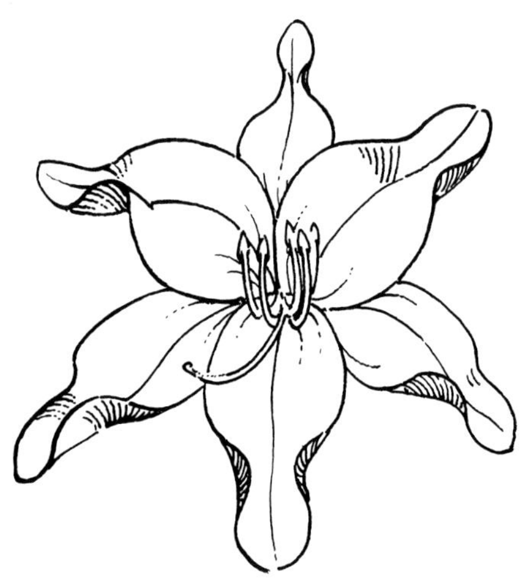

Pinched form

Flower profile

All of the above flower characteristics can be observed by viewing the flower front on. When viewed from the side, other characteristics of flower form and shape can readily be observed. The flower can be described as flat, flaring, recurved, pinched or trumpet-shaped:

- *Flat flowers*—are said to be flat when all of the outer edges of petals and sepals sit roughly in the same plane.
- *Flaring flowers*—are said to be flaring when the segments arch out from the throat as if stretched.
- *Recurved flowers*—basically flare only to have the outer part of the segments roll back beneath the inner parts giving a tucked in effect.
- *Pinched flowers*—have floral parts in two planes and look as though someone has held the flower between two fingers.
- *Trumpet-shaped flowers*—have segments which continue to rise from the throat in an upward line to the point. The parts tend to form the rim of a cup at the outer extremities.

The length and width of the petals and sepals vary to give the shapes described above, from the extremely narrow, open-flowered spiders to those which are extremely wide and full. The sepals are usually narrower than the petals and, at times, we have the pinwheel effect of petals which twist and curl. To all these qualities we can add the distinction of plain (tailored) floral parts or ruffled floral parts. There is endless variation to the flower form and each cultivar has its own distinctive appearance.

Another amazing habit of daylilies is the way the form varies throughout the day as well as from day to day. A good example of this is the beautiful 'Ida Wimberly Munson' which opens very much in a cup-shaped trumpet form and gradually flattens out during the day, whereupon the sepals tend to slightly recurve while the petals take on triangular shape. This daylily flower goes through quite a variety of shapes in its one-day existence and it is beautiful at all stages.

Trumpet form

Substance and texture

There are other issues to discuss when attempting to classify the appearance of a daylily flower. Of significance are the substance and texture of the flower.

Most modern daylilies are heavily substanced and this enables them to withstand the variations in weather to which they are subjected. A poorly substanced flower does not hold well in rain nor will it survive the extreme heat of some summer days and the flower is often well past its best by early to mid afternoon. It is very difficult to classify daylilies according to their substance but it is a point worth mentioning.

Texture of the daylily flower is also variable and it has a definite effect on how one perceives the colour and pattern. The texture can be smooth, rough, waxen or creped:

- *Smooth-textured flowers*—have a brightness and clarity of colour which is most appealing.
- *Rough-textured flowers*—are often overlaid with shadows to give a dramatic effect.
- *Waxen-textured flowers*—have a carved or sculptured appearance giving the impression of heavy substance and great clarity.
- *Crepe-textured flowers*—are very popular. Here the bloom surface is indented, upraised and often rippled to give an appearance similar to crepe paper. These flowers look soft, delicate and of poor substance but have a magical 'different' appeal. In spite of their appearance 'creped' flowers are usually well substanced and hold well in difficult weather conditions.

Flowering time

The period of the day in which the flower is at its peak is a further issue for consideration. Recent hybridising work has extended the bloom period for any particular flower during its one day of existence and there are now daylilies which will last more than 24 hours so that one-day lilies have become two-day lilies. Most daylilies, however, last less than 24 hours and they can be classified according to the time of day in which they are open. The three categories are day-blooming (diurnal), night-blooming (nocturnal) and extended blooming:

- *Diurnal daylilies*—make up the vast majority of registered cultivars. These daylilies open in the morning and are finished the same night (obviously at varying times).
- *Nocturnal daylilies*—open in the evening, flower through the night and into the next day. They are usually spent by midday or early afternoon.
- *Extended blooming*—daylilies are those whose life expectancy approaches or surpasses the full 24 hours. They may flower from one morning through the day and evening until some time the following morning or they may flower from evening through the night and day and close some time in the following afternoon. In general, daylilies are said to have extended bloom if each flower lasts a minimum of 16 hours.

I have found that, in our climate, many daylilies will flower right through into winter and the winter blooms on plants that normally provide only normal lasting flowers will last up to and more than 24 hours. While our daylilies continue to be prolific in winter the flowers lack the intensity of colour found in summer bloom.

Flower colour

The colour range of the daylily flower has been extended in recent times to cover all the basic colours with the exception of blue. From the original species in shades of yellow and orange hybridisers have worked horticultural wonders to produce the magnificent array of colours and patterns now available.

There is a shade of yellow to suit even the most discriminating of collectors. We have palest cream and richest gold and all the imaginable shades of yellow in between. There are orange tones, brown, melon, apricot and tangerine.

Red in all its shades and tonings is available. There are orange-reds, brick reds, real pillar-box red, rose-red, scarlet, maroon and burgundy tones right through to the darkest red which approaches black.

Black daylilies have colours from both the dark purple side and dark red side. All kinds of shades of purple exist with lavender, lilac, mauve and violet through to royal purple with tones that are plum coloured and grape coloured.

In pink there is also a great range from the palest of pale pink through to rich vibrant rose-pink.

White has been an elusive colour, but, in recent years, the white daylilies have reached a level of clarity whereby they can really be called white. Indeed if your fancy does not run exclusively to blue there is sure to be a daylily somewhere to give you pleasure.

'Elizabeth Salter'

'Ruffled Ballet'

'Shirred Lace'

'La Rêve'

'Yazoo Soufflé'

'Test Print'

'Sunset Strut'

'Secret Splendor'

Colour patterns

As well as the basic colour of the daylily flower there are numerous colour patterns. To simplify what has become a very complex issue I wish to divide these colour patterns into six basic divisions while recognising that within each division there are numerous subdivisions. The six basic patterns are:

- Self;
- Blend;
- Polychrome;
- Bicolour;
- Bitone;
- Fancy.

Self

A daylily is called a *self colour* if all the floral parts are of the same single colour

This is an easy definition in theory but, in practice, there are very, very few true self-coloured daylilies in which the whole flower is one solid colour. Most daylilies have a throat whose colour is distinctively different to that of the floral parts. Throat colours are usually in shades of yellow through to orange or green tones so it is basically only in the yellow shades that one can get a pure coloured flower. The size of the throat also varies considerably from cultivar to cultivar. Some are so minute as to have no real visual impact while others are so extended that they can give a bicolour effect on what is basically a self coloured flower.

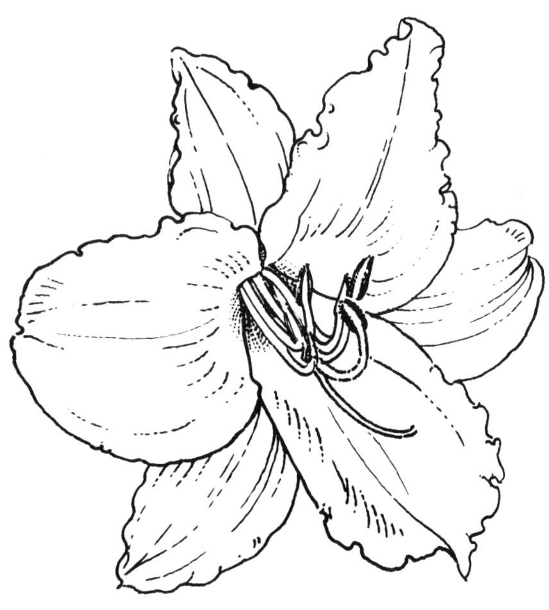

Self pattern

Blend

A *blended flower* is one in which all the floral parts are a mixture of two basic colours or shades of colour.

Blend

Polychrome

A *polychrome flower* is one in which all the floral parts are a mixture of three or more colours or shades of colours.

Polychrome

Bicolour

A *bicolour flower* has sepals of one colour and petals a different colour. If the sepals are lighter than the petals the flower is called bicolour; if the sepals are darker than the petals the flower is said to be a *reverse bicolour*.

Bitone

A *bitone flower* has sepals of one colour and petals a different shade of the same colour. If the sepals are a lighter shade than the petals the flower is called bitone, if the sepals are a darker shade than the petals the flower is said to be a *reverse bitone*.

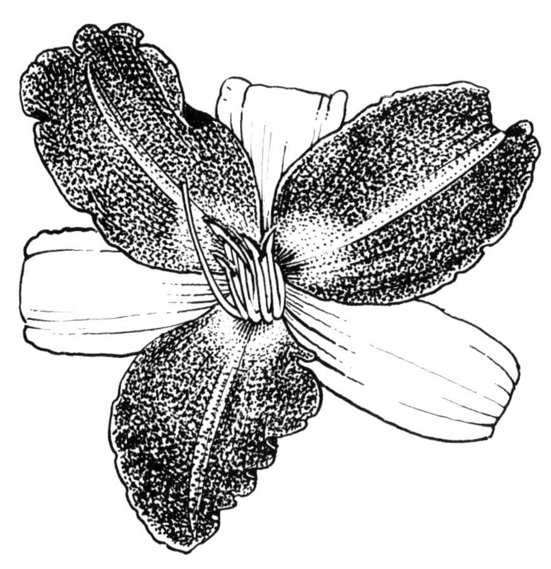

Bicolour

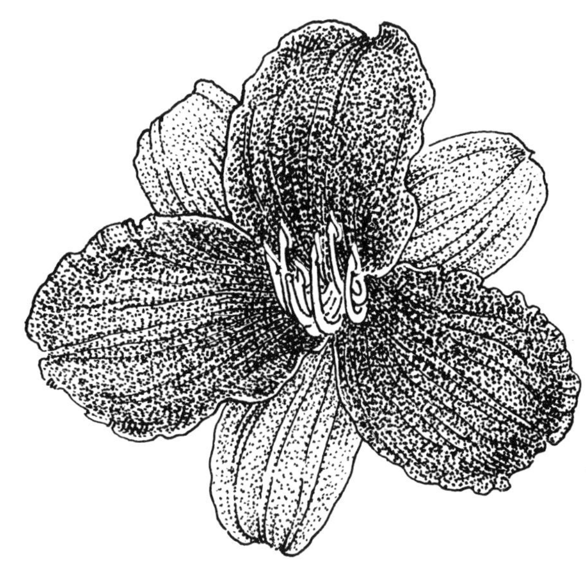

Bitone

Reverse bicolour

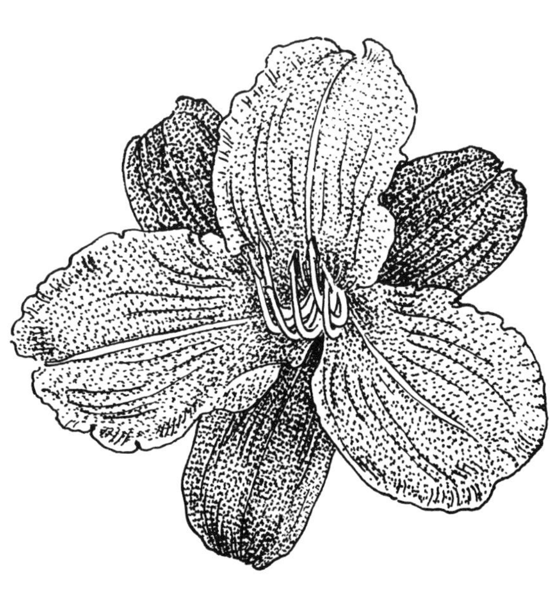

Reverse bitone

Above 'Wings of Tide'

'Snow Bride'

'Vi Simmons'

Left 'Frosted Pink Ice'

'Whooperee'

'Wind Frills'

'Tuscawilla Princess'

'Westminster Lace'

'Victoria's Secret'

Fancy

This is a loose term to define all those daylilies which do not fit into the previous five categories. Many daylilies have additional variations in colour pattern apart from basic colouring. These variations take on various forms, and, with the modern developments, can be most startling and exciting. Once again it is difficult to classify according to these fancy patterns and, at times, the distinction between one pattern and another is not easy to observe.

Eye zones

One of the most common and most beautiful patterns is a ring of colour at the junction of the floral segments and the throat. This 'zone' of colour can take various forms:

The term *eye zone* (or *eyed*) is used if the ring of colour is on both sepals and petals.

Eye zone

The term *band* (or *banded*) is used if the ring of colour is only on the petals.

Band

The term *halo* is used if a band is only slight or barely visible. This usually occurs when the colour of the band is only a different shade of colour to that of the basic petals and not a distinctly different colour. The differentiation between bands and halos can be minimal.

Halo

The term *watermark* is used if a band of colour is very wide and stretches out over most of the petals. Once again, it is usually a different shade of the original colour.

Watermark

In recent times daylilies have been developed with double or even triple eyes of different colours. This trait has been particularly noticeable in the miniature and small-flowered varieties. Again, within these fancy patterns there is great variation in the application of the colour.

Edging

The modern daylily is a gorgeous flower. More and more variations in pattern and colour are being developed for an ever-increasing gardening public. Some daylilies have the flower segments edged in a colour or shade different to that of the basic parts. This edging varies from the thinnest of wire-lines to the clearest of edges up to 1 cm (½ in) width. Colour combinations vary greatly as does the intensity of the colour of this edging. *Picotee edging* describes a line edge of contrasting colour usually on ruffled petals. *Pie-crust edging* is a description used to define very heavily ruffled and indented edges—of the same or different colour to that of the main floral parts. Some daylilies have just the ends of the segments tipped or brushed a colour different to the main part of the segments. This is called *tipping* and can occur on the petals only or on both sepals and petals.

Midrib

Many daylilies have a line of colour down the length of the petals and/or sepals. This is called a midrib and, in some cultivars this midrib is raised above the surface of the rest of the segments. Midrib colours vary, often blending with the main colour and sometimes contrasting vividly.

Dotting

Dotting occurs when the flower has colour spots of varying size and shape on the floral parts. Dotting is not common but can be quite spectacular.

Dusting

Another adornment, and a more common one, is a dusting effect where the surface of the floral parts appears to be coated with sparkling effect. This dusting takes the form of gold dusting where the flowers reflect the light and give a gold sparkle or, more commonly, diamond dusting where the effect is similar but in tones of silver.

Either way, this is a spectacular addition of colour and most daylilies showing this effect are highly prized. Unfortunately, the effect cannot easily be captured on film.

Stamen colour

One last variation in daylilies is seen in the colour of the stamens—the six male parts—which are usually yellow or orange but can vary in colour to be red, black, pink or shades of mauve.

6
Recommended varieties

There is always difficulty in making recommendations of suitable cultivars because there are so many variables, and personal taste is the most important of these variables. A list of recommendations must, by necessity, be a personal selection at a point in time. With the rapid advances being made in the development of the modern daylily and the fads and fashions for colours and patterns continually changing it is no easy task to recommend varieties. Coupled with this is the huge and ever-increasing number of daylilies on the market and the impossibility of seeing them all let alone growing them all. I have restricted myself to a list which encompasses daylilies that I have grown with a very limited few additions that I have observed growing. There will still be notable omissions and some unexpected inclusions. I have not allowed price to enter into my selections—there will be $6 'oldies' in with the $100 plus 'newies' and I realise that cost can be a major factor in the selections that many gardeners make.

In giving descriptions I have tried to use the information provided by the hybridiser as much as possible and have only allowed myself the latitude of minor variations where I saw fit to do so. It must be remembered that daylilies are being hybridised in a wide range of climates and both the height of flowering scape and size of flower will vary according to climate, position in the garden and cultural care. Rate of growth, profusion of flower and recurrence of bloom are also very variable. Remember also that daylilies that are dormant in some climates may be semi-evergreen or even evergreen in warmer climates while the reverse can also be true where daylilies registered as evergreen in warmer climates may be semi-evergreen or dormant in colder climates.

After all of these variables have been noted I should mention that I grow daylilies in a very satisfactory climate and have no difficulty in growing both evergreen and dormant cultivars and a selection from the list provided should give great satisfaction.

Opposite 'Outrageous'

'Ann Blocher'

Large-flowered daylilies

'Admiral's Braid' (Stamile) Ev 52 cm (21 in) Tet M Re Stunning white with a braided gold edge. There is a slight pink blush on the sepals and a slight fragrance can be noted. This is a most beautiful new cultivar with wide well-formed flowers. It has proven to be a good grower and highly productive of bloom. 'Admiral's Braid' has been accepted as one of the best cultivars of recent introduction. It is fertile both ways, i.e. it will set pods from pollen of another cultivar and its own pollen can be used to fertilise another cultivar. *Photo opposite*

'Alec Allen' (Carpenter) Ev 65 cm (26 in) Dip E–M Re Very flat, ruffled and wide-flowered creamy yellow. 'Alec Allen' will re-bloom regularly on well-budded scapes. It is a very good landscaping or mass planting daylily, flowering early and repeating well. The form of the flower is very pleasing and it has vibrancy of colour.

'All American Magic' (Salter) S–Ev 70 cm (28 in) M–L Re Very full, well-formed lavender pink with a wide, heavy gold edge. This daylily was particularly beautiful as seen in Florida and is one of the new heavily ruffled and pie-crust edged cultivars that are so popular. The colour and form of this daylily are both excellent. It is a garden spectacle with smooth substance and wide well-formed petals. *Photo opposite*

'All American Tiger' (Stamile) Ev 60 cm (24 in) Tet E–M Re Beautiful burnt orange with a red eye and red edge and a green throat. Brilliant and unique colour. The blooms are large, rounded, well-formed and held on well-branched scapes. *Photo opposite*

'Alluralee' (Hager) S–Ev 76 cm (30 in) Dip M Re Silk-textured and large-flowered pastel peach self with a green throat. 'Alluralee' grows a little taller than medium height and flowers prolifically throughout the season with many buds. It is good as a specimen or in mass. The vigorous growth, attractive colour and prolific bloom ensure popularity.

'Amber Ballerina' (Munson) S–Ev 50 cm (20 in) Dip E–M Re Amber tones with a gold edge. The blooms are frilled, ruffled and pleated. This is an attractive bloom and a nice contrast with more richly coloured cultivars.

'Amber Lamp' (Munson) Ev 50 cm (20 in) Dip E–M The main features of this daylily are the very large flowers and the creped texture. The colour is a blended amber pink and although this daylily gives only moderate bloom it is spectacular when in flower. It is very popular with garden visitors who are enchanted by the huge spectacular blooms.

'Ann Blocher' (Blocher) S–Ev 50 cm (20 in) Dip E–M Re This has long been a personal favourite. It has medium-sized rosy violet to blue violet flowers with some white in the bloom. Colour varies significantly but is always beautiful. Good for re-bloom and flower production. I have heard and read criticism of this daylily but can never understand why it is not universally loved as I find it a most attractive and distinctly different flower. *Photo opposite*

'Anna's Choice' (Carpenter) Ev 55 cm (22 in) Dip M Re Ruffled peach-pink with a red eye zone. Large flowers are nicely formed and very attractive. This is one of the prettiest of the very popular eyed cultivars.

'Apple Crisp' (Guidry) S–Ev 63 cm (25 in) Dip E–M Re Large ruffled burnt copper and red bitone of good form and excellent garden habits. This daylily is distinctive for its colour.

'Apple Tart' (Hughes) Ev 70 cm (28 in) Tet E–M Re Lightly ruffled mid red with a green throat. Prolific re-bloomer on much taller spikes well over one metre in height. This is a very reliable daylily, tough and prolific. It is spectacular in a clump when established but the individual flowers are of rather ordinary form by modern standards. This is a good daylily to plant in mass at the rear of a display.

'Apricot Wax' (Munson) S–Ev 76 cm (30 in) Tet E–M Re Large, intense apricot self with heavy wax-like substance. This long time favourite is a prolific bloomer, and one of the most popular in its colour range because of its excellent garden habits and prolific bloom.

'Arabian Magic' (Salter) S–Ev 65 cm (26 in) Tet M Re Mid to dark violet-purple with a green heart and a bold silver-white picotee edge. This heavily ruffled and well-formed flower is simply stunning and is a great personal favourite. I fell in love with 'Arabian Magic' when I first saw it in Florida and it has settled in well in Australia. For colour and garden effect it is sensational and will become very popular. The flowers are full and round, the substance is heavy, the scapes are good and it is both vigorous and a good parent. *Photo p.52*

'Aramis' (Benz) Dor 76 cm (30 in) Tet M L Re Rounded, ruffled and frilled brilliant red with a bright green throat. The colour and form of this daylily are outstanding and it will perform well in colder climates. It carries strong, well-branched scapes. The pollen is fertile. *Photo p.52*

'Admiral's Braid'

Above 'All American Magic'

Below 'All American Tiger'

'Arabian Magic'

'Aramis'

'Art Song'

'Aviance'

'Avon Crystal Rose'

'Awash with Colour'

Above 'Aztec Chalice'

Left 'Barbara Mitchell'

Below 'Beauty of Esther'

Right 'Balaringar Promise'

Below 'Beguiled Again'

'Arpeggio' (Kirchoff) Ev 50 cm (20 in) Dip M Re Attractive double in a blend of peach, salmon and ivory. This daylily is consistent, well-branched and prolific. It makes a lovely clump in the garden and is very suitable for mass planting.

'Art Song' (Kirchoff) Ev 60 cm (24 in) Dip E–M Re Peach with a grape-plum eye zone and yellow-green throat. The nicely formed double blooms are carried throughout a long bloom season. *Photo p.52*

'Aviance' (Munson) Ev 50 cm (20 in) Tet E–M Re All-time favourite creamy pink. Flowers are rounded, ruffled and very attractive. Growth and all-round performance are excellent. This is an excellent daylily for landscape work as it blooms well and is most attractive for a massed display in pastel tones of pink. *Photo p.53*

'Avon Crystal Rose' (Moldovan) Dor 65 cm (26 in) Tet M Re Vivid deep rose-pink with an occasional white wire edge. The large flowers are very attractive and this is a garden picture. The rich colour is a magnetic force in attracting people across the garden and it is well worth growing for colour alone. *Photo p.53*

'Awash with Colour' (Stamile) Ev 80 cm (32 in) Tet E–M Re Very beautiful blend of rose, pink, lavender and soft violet. Large flowers on super scapes, well-branched and multi-budded. The plant is vigorous, the flower is fragrant and this daylily is fertile. *Photo p.53*

'Aztec Chalice' (Hager) Ev 88 cm (35 in) Tet M Re Recurved bright red of nice form and excellent colour. Growth is very good. The brilliant red colour and unusual but attractive shape of the flowers make this a standout. *Photo p.54*

'Balaringar Promise' (Lee) Ev 85 cm (34 in) Dip E–M–L Re This is the loveliest of Margaret Lee's daylilies, a beautiful clear light pink with deeper veins and a green throat. The medium-sized flowers are ruffled and diamond-dusted. Excellent growth. This is probably the best Australian raised cultivar currently available and it is an excellent garden performer over a long bloom period. It is a landscaping spectacle. *Photo p.55*

'Ballerina Princess' (Hite) Dor 80 cm (32 in) Tet M Pastel pink blend which is large and ruffled. The blooms are attractive and this is a suitable plant for colder climates where it performs well. This cultivar is a long-term favourite.

'Balls of Red' Dor 76 cm (30 in) Dip M Re An old but very good red double which is reliable and prolific. It has excellent garden value as a clump where it lives up to its name—literally covered in balls of red.

'Banana Republic' (Salter) S–Ev to Ev 65 cm (26 in) Tet M Re Very large flowers, well-formed and attractive in colouring. Pale lemon overlaid peach pink with a large green throat and a light rose-red pencil etched eye. Prolific bloomer with many flowers open simultaneously. Although this daylily is pastel in colour it is a garden standout with its huge flowers and the sheer quantity of bloom produced. It is very popular with visitors who are drawn to it by the mass of bloom. It is an excellent parent for large flowers with eye patterns and is very fertile. *Photo p.2*

'Barbara Mitchell' (Pierce) S–Ev to Dor 60 cm (24 in) Dip M Re Gorgeous, rounded and ruffled pink with a green throat. Wide overlapping petals and superb form. This is an outstanding daylily in every way and is deservedly popular. It will be grown with pride for many years. 'Barbara Mitchell' is one of the top three daylilies grown in the USA and will be equally popular in Australian when better known. It has proven an easy grower and is a garden spectacle. *Photo p.54*

'Beauty of Esther' (Jinkerson) Ev 68 cm (27 in) Tet M Large, wide, flat and ruffled blooms are flesh pink with darker overtones. The quality of bloom and growth are both excellent and this is one of the most liked daylilies with visitors to the garden. It is a very easy and most rewarding daylily to grow. *Photo p.54*

'Beauty To Behold' (Sellers) S–Ev 60 cm (24 in) Dip M Light yellow with a green throat. This very tough and reliable daylily is outstanding in a clump and provides a mass of bloom when in flower. It is an excellent plant for mass display.

'Beguiled Again' (Salter) Ev 75 cm (30 in) Tet M–L Re Lovely mid lavender-purple with a large cream throat, deep green heart and bright gold edge. The flowers are well-formed and heavily ruffled. Quality is excellent. This daylily is new and is excellent for individual specimen planting. It has smooth substance, is vigorous and opens well. It is fertile and a parent for gold edges. *Photo p.55*

Above 'Benchmark'

Left 'Betty Woods'

Below 'Big Target'

'Black Ambrosia'

Left 'Bill Norris'

'Blue Happiness'

Opposite 'Blonde Is Beautiful'

'Bel Air Dawn' (Salter) S–Ev 70 cm (28 in) Tet M–L Re Pale pink with a lime-green throat. Colour is pure and the large flowers are very well-formed. This is a most attractive soft coloured daylily and is one of the best of the pure pastel pinks. It is fertile and a good parent.

'Benchmark' (Munson) Ev 75 cm (30 in) Tet M Re One of the first of the large, well-formed lavenders and still well worth growing. It is a clear lavender with lighter midribs and a cream throat. The flowers have excellent substance and bloom is prolific. When first released this was the benchmark for lavender-toned daylilies. It is an outstanding garden performer and is very fertile. *Photo p.57*

'Betty Warren Woods' (Munson) Ev 60 cm (24 in) Tet E–M Re Medium-sized flowers are creamy yellow with a yellow flush and a gold edge. The flowers are well-formed, ruffled and carried in profusion. This is an outstanding daylily for colour and form and has been used extensively in the breeding campaigns of the leading hybridisers.

'Betty Woods' (Kirchoff) Ev 65 cm (26 in) Dip E Re This is one of the best double-flowered daylilies and an all-time favourite. Large brilliant yellow flowers are carried in profusion over a long bloom season. The flowers are fragrant and have a green throat. Betty Woods is deservedly very popular as it is such a good garden performer, outstanding in a clump or for massed display. *Photo p.57*

'Big Target' (Hansen) S–Ev 75 cm (30 in) Dip EM Re Very large, well-formed flowers are yellow with a wide red eye zone and a dark green throat. It was most beautiful as seen in the hybridiser's garden in Florida and has proven very adaptable in a wide range of climates. The colouring is more subtle than startling but the visual effect is most pleasing. *Photo p.57*

'Bill Norris' (Kirchoff) Ev 78 cm (31 in) Tet M Re This has to be close to being the most beautifully formed of all daylilies. The rounded, ruffled flowers are a rich golden-yellow with great clarity of colour. Blooms are large, fragrant and produced over a long period. 'Bill Norris' has settled in well in Australia and when better distributed will take its place as one of the great daylilies. It has everything going for it with well-branched, multi-budded scapes. It is vigorous, very fertile and an excellent parent. *Photo p.58*

'Black Ambrosia' (Salter) S–Ev 75 cm (30 in) Tet M Re Large, velvet-textured rich dark purple very near black with a bright green throat. This new daylily is proving a good grower and the ruffled, rounded flowers are sensational. It was a garden spectacle as seen in the hybridiser's garden in Florida and will be highly acclaimed when distributed in Australia. *Photo p.58*

'Blazing Flame' (Guidry) S–Ev 48 cm (19 in) Dip M Re Large, wide and ruffled rose-red bitone with excellent plant habits. The colour of this daylily is very attractive and it is popular in the garden.

'Blessed Trinity' (Monette) S–Ev 50 cm (20 in) Dip E Re Large, flat and rounded near white with a green throat. This daylily is a lovely one in a clump and although it is an older variety it retains its garden value both for its colour and all-round performance.

'Blonde Is Beautiful' (Harris) S–Ev to Ev 70 cm (28 in) Tet M Re One of the nicest lemon-yellow daylilies with large, flat and ruffled blooms. The quality is excellent and bloom is prolific over an extended period. In a colour class that is somewhat overcrowded this daylily retains both its individuality and its appeal. It will remain a firm favourite. *Photo p.59*

'Blue Happiness' (Spalding) S–Ev 53 cm (21 in) Dip E Absolutely gorgeous clear smooth rose-pink of impeccable form and colour. This is a long-time favourite pink. Why the name 'Blue'? It is certainly not blue but one of the nicest shades of bright pink. Although it is very sparse for re-bloom it is a garden spectacle in the main bloom season. *Photo p.58*

'Bookmark' (Munson) Ev 60 cm (24 in) Tet E–M Re Ruffled salmon-pink with pink highlights. Large flowers of quality, prolific bloom and excellent plant habits. Flowers are often recurved and are always attractive in a colour that is very popular. This is one of the really good landscaping daylilies. *Photo p.63*

'Brand New Lover' (Brooks) S–Ev 70 cm (28 in) Tet E–M Re Lovely coral-rose bitone with a rose halo and a crinkled gold edge. This beautiful daylily has large flowers and prolific bloom. It is top quality in every respect and is a most commanding plant when in bloom. *Photo p.61*

Opposite 'Brand New Lover'

'Brown Eyed Girl'

'Brandenburg'

'Charles Johnston'

'Canton Harbor'

Left 'Champagne Elegance'

Below 'Bookmark'

'China Crystal'

'Cherished Treasure'

'China Lake'

'Brandenburg' (Munson) Ev 65 cm (26 in) Tet E–M Re Large, broad pastel lilac-orchid to lavender with a cream throat and chartreuse heart. This daylily has excellent plant habits and prolific bloom. It is similar to 'Benchmark' in colour and form and there is little to differentiate between these two fine cultivars. *Photo p.62*

'Brown Eyed Girl' (Kirchoff) Ev 65 cm (26 in) Tet E–M Re Basic colour is orange-apricot with a large eye zone of hazelnut-chocolate and a gold-green throat. Blooms are large, ruffled and rounded. Scapes are excellent as is the re-bloom. This is a new daylily and one that is both distinctly different and very popular. *Photo p.62*

'Bunny Eyes' (Kirchoff) Ev 70 cm (28 in) Tet M Re Large-flowered, bright peach-pink with a rose-red eye zone and yellow to green throat. There is a rose-red edge to the bloom and the form is wide and full. Scapes are strong and well branched.

'Burning Inheritance' (Salter) S–Ev 75 cm (30 in) Tet M Re Very bright, intensely coloured orange-red with a small lime heart. Large, well-formed blooms create a colour spectacle as seen in Florida. It is new to Australia but has settled in well and should be very popular. The substance is smooth and holds well. It carries excellent scapes.

'Canadian Border Patrol' (Salter) Ev 75 cm (30 in) Tet M Re Of all the picotee-edged varieties this is a favourite. The base colour is ivory-white with a deep purple eye and a deep purple ruffled picotee edge and a small lime green throat. Large flowers and sensational colour. When seen in Florida this was an eye-catching standout and it is proving to be a very good performer. It will be a wonderful specimen plant. The substance is smooth and heavy and the scapes are well branched. It grows well.

'Cantique' (Bryant) S–Ev 55 cm (22 in) Dip M This is a lovely rounded clear pink flower on one of the quickest of all daylilies to increase. It couples health with vigour and is a desirable landscape or garden plant. Unfortunately it blooms only in the main season but it is prolific when in bloom.

'Canton Harbor' (Munson) Ev 80 cm (32 in) Tet E–M Re I love the coral-orange daylilies which have—as I call them—sunset colours and this is one of the best in that colour range. The large flowers are flat and ruffled. Bloom is prolific with very good re-bloom. 'Canton Harbor' is a very good daylily for landscaping or individual specimen planting. *Photo p.63*

'Carolicolossal' (Powell) S–Ev 90 cm (36 in) Dip E Re Huge spidery yellow-green flowers. This is one of the better spider types which holds itself better than most and is generous in its bloom.

'Casino Gold' (Brooks) S–Ev 80 cm (32 in) Tet EM Re Large, round, ruffled light yellow-gold which has a long bloom season. The attractive flowers are very rounded and most attractive in a clump.

'Casual Pleasure' (Gates) Ev 55 cm (22 in) Tet E Re Large-flowered and well-formed lavender-pink blend with a green throat. The blooms are fragrant and the production is prolific. In a crowded class this is a distinctive flower of quality.

'Celestial Peach' (Kirchoff) Ev 60 cm (24 in) Tet VE Re Very ruffled peach-pink to rose-pink with a gold edge. Large rounded blooms are produced throughout the season. There is a glow about this daylily that sets it apart and makes it stand out when it blooms. Although new to the garden in Dural it has performed very well.

'Celestial Virtue' (Salter) S–Ev 70 cm (28 in) Tet M–L Re Large, full rose-pink with a green throat of good quality. The ruffled blooms are recurrent and the plant habits are very good. It is well branched and carries multiple blooms. Fertile both ways.

'Chamonix' (Munson) Ev 76 cm (30 in) Tet E–M Ruffled blend of rose, pink and yellow with large blooms on excellent scapes and vigorous plants. 'Chamonix' has been an extremely popular daylily because of its outstanding garden performance. Many flowers are produced in a clump.

'Champagne Elegance' (Brown) Ev Dip 73 cm (29 in) E–M Re Absolutely gorgeous wide, full-formed and ruffled cream, near white with a tiny green throat. This was sensational in the hybridiser's garden in Florida and has settled in well in Australia. The very rounded and heavily ruffled blooms are a standout in any daylily planting and this is destined to be highly popular when well distributed. *Photo p.63*

'Charles Johnston' (Gates) S–Ev to Dor 60 cm (24 in) Tet E–M Re Wide, flat and ruffled cherry-red with a lime-green throat. The fragrant blooms are large and imposing while growth is excellent. This is an outstanding daylily, if given some protection from the hot sun as it is inclined to 'grease' in very hot conditions. In a suitable position this daylily is a colour gem. *Photo p.62*

'Christmas Is.'

Left 'Cortez Cove'

Below 'Clairvoyant Lady'

'Cosmic Caper'

Right 'Cindy's Eye'

Below right 'Coral Moon'

Below 'Collier'

'Charlie Pierce Memorial' (Wilson) S–Ev to Ev 60 cm (24 in) Dip E–M Re Of all the lavender-toned daylilies this is a personal favourite. Large ruffled clear lavender with a purple eye and a green throat. Great colour, lovely bloom, prolific plant and very healthy growth ensure that this daylily will be one of the most popular. It is outstanding in every way, as a garden specimen, for an extended planting or for massed display.

'Chemistry' (Blyth) Ev 76 cm (30 in) Tet E–M Re Vibrant autumn-toned beauty in a blend of coral, salmon and apricot. Bloom is prolific and plant habits are excellent, making this one of the top daylilies in sunset colours. It is a very good landscaping daylily. *Photo p.36*

'Cherished Treasure' (Munson) Ev 76 cm (30 in) Tet E–M Re Large yellow washed peach with a yellow-green throat. The fragrant blooms are nicely formed and quite pretty. *Photo p.64*

'Cherry Chapeau' (Munson) Ev 70 cm (28 in) Tet E–M Re Very beautiful bicolour in cream and rose-red. Blooms are ruffled and large. The plant is floriferous and growth is excellent, the bloom is distinctive in colouring that is most attractive and still this daylily has not had the popularity it deserves. I find this difficult to understand as this is a very worthy plant, both as a specimen and for massed display.

'Cherry Eyed Pumpkin' (Kirchoff) S–Ev 70 cm (28 in) Tet VE Re Nicely rounded flowers are orange with a dark red eye zone and often with a red picotee edge. The flowers are produced over a long bloom period and are of a distinctive and vibrant colour that ensures appeal. This is one of the nicest eyed cultivars.

'Chestnut Mountain' (Salter) S–Ev 70 cm (28 in) Tet M Re Bright gold with a tan overlay gives a light but bright brown effect in the garden. The heavily ruffled, large flowers carry a gold edge. This is a very attractive daylily in subtle and distinctive tones. It has beautiful rounded form and is a great foil for the rich dark colours.

'China Crystal' (Moldovan) Dor 70 cm (28 in) Tet M Re Creamy pink blend with a ruffled gold wire edge. This daylily is large, broad and well-formed. It has a certain glow—a crystal-like sheen to the petals—that sets it apart. It is an excellent performer in cold climates. *Photo p.64*

'China Lake' (Munson) S–Ev 70 cm (28 in) Tet E–M Re One of the all-time top daylilies! Rosy lilac flowers have a green throat, are large and produced in abundance. This is the daylily that beckons people across the garden and is outstanding in every way. Visitors cannot resist the rich gorgeous colour and superb plant habits. It is a 'must' for any collection and a great personal favourite. The plant is vigorous and the scapes are excellent. *Photo p.64*

'Chinese Cloisonné' (Munson) S–Ev 70 cm (28 in) Tet E–M Re Everyone is attracted to this daylily because of its unusual colour pattern of creamy melon with a blue-violet eye edged in plum-violet. Large flowers of unusual fluted form set it apart as distinctive. It grows and flowers well.

'Chinese New Year' (Woodhall) Dor 70 cm (28 in) Tet E–M Re Red-orange flowers are ruffled and large. The bloom has quality and production is good. The vibrant colour is a beacon across the garden and this daylily should grow well in colder climates. *Photo p.37*

'Chinese Scholar' (Salter) S–Ev 55 cm (22 in) Tet M Re Large red double with a gold edge. The quality bloom is consistently double and although new to Australia the plant is growing well and this should be a popular red double.

'Chinese Temple Flower' (Munson) Ev 80 cm (32 in) Tet E–M Re Lilac-lavender with a darker band around a cream throat. Excellent growth and good bloom production together with distinctive colouration ensure deserved popularity for this plant.

'Chris Salter' (Salter) S–Ev 65 cm (26 in) Tet E–M Re Mid lavender with a very heavily ruffled gold picotee edge. The medium to large flowers are of sensational colour and form. It is a most stunning bloom and a clump in full bloom is a sight worth seeing. Growth and vigour are good and this new cultivar has already attracted much attention.

'Christmas Day' (Blyth) Dor 95 cm (38 in) Tet E Re Large, imposing vibrant blood-red with a slightly darker red-black eye zone. This is a very beautiful daylily which first opened and was seen by the hybridiser on Christmas Day—hence the name. Being dormant it is an outstanding plant for colder climates but it is such an easy grower that it is worth its place in any collection. With me, it was love at first sight and this love has endured. *Photo on front cover*

'Christmas Is.' (Yancey) Dor 65 cm (26 in) Dip E–M Re Medium-sized flowers are bright red with a huge bright green throat spilling right out on to the petals. This colour gem remains one of the most popular daylilies because of the large amount of green in the flower and the beautiful contrast in colour. *Photo p.66*

'Cindy's Eye' (Salter) S–Ev 75 cm (30 in) Tet E–M Re Very beautiful cream to ivory with a large lavender-purple eye and picotee edge. The large flowers are well-formed and exquisitely patterned. This is one of the best of the picotees and will be very popular when well distributed. The plant is vigorous and the flower is showy. It is fertile and an excellent parent. *Photo p.67*

'Clairvoyant Lady' (Hansen) S–Ev 55 cm (22 in) Dip L Re Light violet with a big purple eye zone. The medium-sized flowers are produced in abundance and are of unique colouration. I loved this daylily when I saw it in the hybridiser's garden in Florida and now grow it and enjoy it. *Photo p.66*

'Classy Cast' (Brooks) S–Ev 76 cm (30 in) Tet M Re Large wax-textured light coral-rose with a green throat. The ruffled blooms are a delightful soft colour with a glow or 'cast' that is most attractive. Growth habits are excellent and this is a very pleasing daylily.

'Claudine' (Millikan) Dor 60 cm (24 in) Tet M Attractive bloom in rich blood-red with a darker eye zone. The large flowers are rounded and ruffled. Growth is excellent and, being dormant, this is a valuable plant for colder climates.

'Cleda Jones' (Chesnik) S–Ev 76 cm (30 in) Tet E–M Re Flat, rounded, ruffled and full-formed, clear golden-yellow of heavy substance and excellent quality. This is one of the best yellows for garden display and is outstanding for landscape work as all its garden habits are excellent. In a very crowded class this is one of the best. *Photo p.33*

'Collier' (Brown) S–Ev 70 cm (28 in) Tet E–M Re Gorgeous wide-petalled blend of pink, gold, cream and yellow with a tiny green throat. Rounded, ruffled blooms have corduroy texture. This is an outstanding new daylily which was 'oh, so beautiful' in the hybridiser's garden and is 'oh, so beautiful' in the garden at Dural. For form and colour it is a personal favourite and it is fertile. *Photo p.67*

'Colour Man' (Blyth) Ev 90cm Tet E–M Re Ruffled pure orange with a red-orange halo. Nicely rounded blooms are freely produced and this is an excellent daylily for massed garden display or landscaping.

'Comanche Eyes' (Guidry) Ev 76 cm (30 in) Dip E Re Large, ruffled, creamy peach-pink with a rose-red halo. Flower production is good and quality is very good. The colour is subtle rather than startling and the plant is attractive.

'Cool Jazz' (Kirchoff) Ev 70 cm (28 in) Tet E Re Large, clear light pink with wide overlapping petals, ruffled and edged in gold. This prolific daylily is deservedly very popular and is a garden spectacle in pastel tones when in bloom. It has excellent plant habits.

'Coral Autumn' (Kirchoff) Ev 60 cm (24 in) Tet M Re This is a beautiful blend of peach, coral and rose with a yellow halo and green throat. The nicely rounded flowers are, at times, double and often are both double and single on the same scape when established. Beautiful daylily!

'Coral Moon' (Munson) Ev 70 cm (28 in) Tet M Re This rounded rich pastel blend of coral and pink is a personal favourite. The bloom is prolific and the quality is superb. It is one of the best daylilies for all-round performance and is most suitable for landscaping or specimen planting. *Photo p.67*

'Corelli' (Munson) Ev 45 cm (18 in) Tet M L Pastel blend of peach-pink and yellow with a deeper halo and green throat. The large blooms are nicely ruffled, and this is one of the prettiest pastels.

'Cortez Cove' (Roberts) Ev 70 cm (28 in) Tet M Re This greenish yellow daylily is set apart from others by the textured blooms which give a most desirable effect. The rounded blooms are large and produced over a great length of time. This is excellent! 'Cortez Cove' is a distinctive daylily in a cluttered class and is most suitable for specimen planting or in the landscape. *Photo p.66*

'Cosmic Caper' (Harris-Benz) Ev 60 cm (24 in) Tet M–L Lavender with a darker halo. Blooms are large, heavily ruffled and have a fringed, knobby border. This daylily is attractive and distinctive. It is particularly nice when grown with lemon-toned daylilies and, although not registered as a re-bloomer, it does regularly re-bloom for us. *Photo p.67*

Above 'Court Magician'

Above left 'Cotton Club'

Left 'Dancing with Pink'

'Dazzle'

'Devonshire'

'De Colores'

Right 'Easy Ned'

'Daring Dilemma'

'Cotton Club' (Kirchoff) Ev 50 cm (20 in) Dip E–M Re Pastel amber to butter-cream double of quality. The blooms are full, ruffled and consistently double once established. Plant habits are very good for growth, health and vigour. *Photo p. 70*

'Court Magician' (Munson) Ev 75 cm (30 in) Tet E–M Re Rich lavender-purple with a chalky lavender eye and a large yellow-green throat. The medium to large-sized flowers are very colourful and this is a lovely daylily. Because of its spectacular colour this daylily is outstanding as a specimen plant. It grows well. *Photo p. 70*

'Crazy Pierre' (Whitacre) S–Ev 60 cm (24 in) Dip M Large cream spider with a red centre. This is one of the better performing spiders as the scapes are reasonably strong.

'Creative Edge' (Stamile) Ev 58 cm (23 in) (23 in) Tet M Re Very ruffled creamy lavender with a purple eye and purple picotee edge surrounded by pie-crust gold. When established the flowers have gold knobs to add to their splendour. Most unusual and most attractive as a specimen plant because of its unique colouration. It has excellent substance and is fertile.

'Czar's Treasure' (Munson) Ev 60 cm (24 in) Tet M Re Orchid with a cream halo. Attractive medium-sized flowers are produced in profusion and this is an excellent pastel-toned daylily, very suitable for massed display.

'Daisy' (Glidden) Ev 76 cm (30 in) Dip E M Large greenish spider with a lavender influence and a large green throat. Nice spider type but stems are weak and it needs staking.

'Dance Ballerina Dance' (Peck) Dor 50 cm (20 in) Tet M Re Melon-apricot of great quality and has been much used a parent. Rounded, ruffled blooms need heat to open well. When at its best this is a very attractive flower but it is often poorly formed unless the nights are hot. It is more renowned as a quality parent than as a garden plant. There are many better garden performers in this colour range.

'Dancing With Pink' (Kirchoff) Ev 58 cm (23 in) Dip E–M Re Beautiful, soft, pastel pink double with a porcelain sheen. The flowers are full, rounded and ruffled and the quality is superb. I loved this daylily in the hybridiser's garden and now grow it with pride as it performs very well in the garden and is most attractive on re-bloom. *Photo p. 70*

'Daring Dilemma' (Salter) S–Ev to Ev 75 cm (30 in) Tet M Re Cream shaded pink with a plum-purple eye and edge. The medium to large flowers are rounded, heavily ruffled and well-formed. Growth is excellent, bloom is prolific and it is a garden spectacle. One of the very best! Because of its outstanding performance and attractive colour 'Daring Dilemma' can be recommended as one of the top few classic daylilies. It is fertile and a proven parent. *Photo p. 71*

'David Kirchoff' (Salter) S–Ev 70 cm (28 in) Tet M Re Lavender with a bold wide gold edge. Stunning, large flower of excellent form and beautiful colour. I loved this daylily when I first saw it but, as I have not grown it, I cannot report on its garden performance. It is sufficient praise for me to list it without having grown it. *Photo p. 14*

'Dazzle' (Hansen) S–Ev 55 cm (22 in) Dip L Re Attractive small-flowered orchid lavender with a purple eye zone. First released as a companion for 'Razzle' so you can have 'razzle dazzle' in the garden with two distinctly different eyed cultivars. *Photo p. 70*

'De Colores' (Temple) Ev 70 cm (28 in) Dip E Re Huge multicoloured spider in bright yellow, tan and rose. Red-purple eye zone and large green throat set off the medley of colours. Well-branched, multi-budded and consistent in bloom, this is an outstanding spider type with blooms around 25 cm (10 in) from tip to tip. Great for spider lovers. *Photo p. 71*

'Delicate Treasure' (Munson) S–Ev 70 cm (28 in) Tet E M Blend of cream and shades of pink. Wide, ruffled flowers, soft in colour but vibrant, are produced in profusion. This is lovely in a clump and is an outstanding pastel for massed display and landscaping. 'Delicate Treasure' is a long-time, high quality special daylily.

'Devonshire' (Munson) Ev 76 cm (30 in) Tet E–M Re Very large ivory-yellow with a lacy yellow-gold edge. The flower is stunning, growth is very good and production of bloom excellent. Superb daylily in every respect and ideal for specimen planting or landscaping. *Photo p. 70*

'Divine Madness' (Munson) S–Ev to Dor 50 cm (20 in) Tet M Re Bright red-orange with a copper influence. These large heavily ruffled flowers are fluted and crimped and very attractive. It is certainly one of the better new daylilies in a class that has many competitors. *Photo p. 74*

'Double Conch Shell' (Stamile) Ev 65 cm (26 in) Dip E M Pale melon double of pretty, ruffled form. Grows well and is consistently good in the garden. This will be very popular when it is more widely grown. *Photo p. 74*

'Double Cranberry Ruffles' (Talbot) S–Ev 48 cm (19 in) Dip M–L Large double cranberry-red with a green throat. The blooms are ruffled and fragrant. I loved this daylily as seen in the hybridiser's garden but have had no personal experience in growing it. *Photo p. 74*

'Double Pink Treasure' (Brown) S–Ev 53 cm (21 in) Dip M Gorgeous double creamy pink flowers are a delight. Bloom is large, production is excellent. This is a very reliable pink double and one of the all-time favourites. The pink colouration is not intense but the overall effect is subtle and beautiful. Garden habits are exemplary. *Photo p. 74*

'Drop Cloth' (Salter) S–Ev 70 cm (28 in) Tet M Re Pale ivory-cream overlaid with stipples and spots of maroon. Small yellow-green throat and thin gold edge. Round, ruffled blooms are unique for colour and pattern and this is worth growing as a talking point if nothing else. The pattern is very similar to the plicata pattern found in bearded iris. *Photo p. 75*

'Dynasty Pink' (Kirchoff) Ev 70 cm (28 in) Tet E–M Re Large, wide flowers are smooth icy pink with overlapping rolled-back form. This daylily has good bud count and plentiful re-bloom. I just loved this daylily as seen in the hybridiser's Florida garden and I have found it to be equally beautiful in Dural. It is a very good pink.

'Earth Angel' (Sellers) Ev 76 cm (30 in) Tet M Re One of the very best apricot daylilies. The large flowers are of excellent quality and are produced in profusion from excellent plants. This is a super quality daylily for massed display and is a landscaper special. *Photo p. 75*

'Easy Ned' (B. Brown) Ev 100 cm (40 in) Dip VL Spider-type chartreuse self with a green throat. Large flowers on tall scapes and the flowers are held reasonably well. *Photo p. 71*

'Ed Kirchoff' (Kirchoff) S–Ev 58 cm (23 in) Tet E Re This smooth saffron yellow with great carrying power is a long-time favourite. The blooms are ruffled and have a pie-crust edge. This is a landscaping masterpiece, particularly useful for massed, low-growing display. *Photo p. 74*

'Ed Murray' (Grovatt) S–Ev 95 cm (38 in) Dip E–M Re Very tall-growing dark black-red self of ruffled form and bountiful bloom. Quality daylily if you like tall growth but the scapes often tower above the foliage. It is quite popular.

'Egyptian Ibis' (Munson) S–Ev 65 cm (26 in) Tet E–M Re Silvery lilac with a large green throat. The large ruffled flowers are carried on excellent scapes. This is a very beautiful cultivar of lovely, delicate colour and its plant habits are excellent. *Photo p. 75*

'Eighteen Karat' (Brown) S–Ev 63 cm (25 in) (25 in) Tet E–M Re Very large bright golden-yellow flowers in profusion result in this being a great favourite. Excellent plant habits and productivity make this a landscaping special. This is a standout in an overcrowded class and is one of the top ten daylilies that we grow. *Photo p. 75*

'El Rosario' (Peck) Dor 65 cm (26 in) Tet E–M Wide, ruffled rose-pink bitone of quality. This daylily is unique in its colouring and garden effect and it performs well in a wide range of climates. It has only one round of bloom but is spectacular when it is in flower.

'El Tigre' (Durio) Ev 76 cm (30 in) Tet E–M Re Large, rounded, bright tangerine with an olive-green throat and darker eye zone. Garden performance is good and this daylily has retained its popularity. *Photo p. 75*

'Elizabeth Salter' (Salter) S–Ev 55 cm (22 in) Tet M Re Pale melon to melon-pink with a lime-green heart. Very heavily substanced, large, rounded and ruffled blooms are a garden spectacle. This is one of the all-time great daylilies, spectacular in every way. I thought this was one of the top few daylilies that I saw in the USA and now that I grow it myself, its standing has even improved. I rate 'Elizabeth Salter' as one of the top few daylilies in cultivation. It is particularly pretty on re-bloom. Branching is excellent and it has fertile pollen although pods are difficult to set. *Photo p. 40*

'Elles' (Spalding) Ev 53 cm (21 in) Dip M Sensational, large, ruffled bright pink with darker ribbed veins. Unfortunately, the blooms are very prone to attacks by thrips but, if kept clean, they are among the very best. I have always loved this daylily but find it difficult to keep it clean. Thrip free flowers are sensational.

'Divine Madness'

'Double Pink Treasure'

'Ed Kirchoff'

'Double Conch Shell'

'Double Cranberry Ruffles'

'Earth Angel'

'Drop Cloth'

'El Rosario'

'Egyptian Ibis'

'Eighteen Karat'

'Eloquent Silence' (Salter) S–Ev 70 cm (28 In) Tet M Re Pale ivory to white with a large ruffled gold edge and a small green throat. The very large flowers are wide, ruffled and of outstanding form. The delicate colouring makes this a most desirable daylily. Scapes are good and it is proving fertile and an excellent parent. When better known, this most beautiful daylily will be very popular. *Photo p.78*

'Enchanted Empress' (Munson) Ev 48 cm (19 in) Dip E–M Creamy lavender-pink of full form and pretty colouration. The large flowers are fragrant and are produced in a massed display early in the season. It is a most useful cultivar for massed display in pastel colours.

'Enduring Love' (B. Brown) Ev 48 cm (19 in) Dip E–M Spidery light cream with a wide purple eye. The flowers are very large and hence have appeal for those who like narrow segments. *Photo p.36*

'Erica Nicole Gonzales' (Spalding-Guillory) Ev 48 cm (19 in) Dip E–M Re Beautiful lavender with a darker eye. The attractive heavily ruffled and rounded blooms are unique because of the texture veining and colouration. This is a special daylily for lovers of the unusual. I have found the beautiful colour pattern to be very popular. *Photo p.78*

'Etosha' (Munson) Ev 76 cm (30 in) Tet E–M Re Large blended flower of orange, coral and rose. The quality rounded and ruffled flowers are produced in profusion. This is a special daylily for colour, flower production and plant habit. It is a personal favourite in colour pattern and tones so special to daylily colours. *Photo p.78*

'Evening Enchantment' (Stamile) Ev 65 cm (26 in) Tet E–M Re Rich, deep, clear purple with a green throat. Blooms are wide, round and heavily ruffled. Scapes are well branched and multi-budded. Fertile. *Photo p.78*

'Ever So Ruffled' (Stamile) S–Ev 68 cm (27 in) Tet E M Re This is one of the great daylilies! Bloom is deep yellow with sparkling deeply ruffled edges. Flowers are large, rounded and of outstanding form. Everything about this daylily is quality and it ranks as one of the very best for specimen planting, massed display or landscaping. It is also fertile. *Photo p.21*

'Extra Strokes' (Brown) S–Ev 70 cm (28 in) Dip E–M Super ruffled yellow-gold-peach blend of quality. This daylily was a delight as seen in the hybridiser's garden and should be a worthy addition to the daylilies grown in Australia. *Photo p.78*

'Eyed Radiance' (Carpenter) Ev 60 cm (24 in) Dip M Re Pastel creamy peach with a large striking red eye zone. Quality flower on a quality plant that really grows. This is one of the best fancy eyed varieties and is a garden spectacle. It is outstanding for bloom and performance and is superb in a massed display. *Photo p.78*

'Fairytale Pink' (Pierce) S–Ev to Dor 60 cm (24 in) Dip M–L Re Pastel pink with a green throat. Lovely form and excellent plant habits accompanied by prolific bloom have ensured this daylily has continuing popularity. When in flower it is an absolute mass of bloom. *Photo p.79*

'Fantasy Quilt' (Morss) Ev 70 cm (28 in) Tet E Re Large pale ivory with a burgundy-purple eye zone and purple picotee edge and yellow-green throat. This nicely coloured daylily produces plentiful re-bloom and is a most attractive garden spectacle. *Photo p.79*

'Father Fidalis' (Durio) Ev 70 cm (28 in) Tet E–M Re Bright yellow with white midribs. The very large blooms are ruffled and consistently produced. This easy growing daylily is excellent for landscaping or massed display.

'Feathered Angel' (Kirchoff) S–Ev 68 cm (27 in) Tet E–M Re Beautiful blend of honey, cantaloupe, pink and gold with a gold filigree edge. This well-formed daylily is a gorgeous colour with most impressive form. It was superb as seen in the hybridiser's Florida garden and already has made an excellent impression in Australia.

'Femme Osage' (Whatley) S–Ev 63 cm (25 in) Tet M Light melon-tangerine of rich dazzling colour. The flowers are large, wide, ruffled, crimped and scalloped. The form is unusual but the garden effect is great and the plant grows and flowers well. *Photo p.78*

'Fiesta Fling' (Brown) S–Ev 70 cm (28 in) Tet M–L Re This is a large, wide and crepe-textured rosy pink bitone with lighter midribs and a rose eye. The blooms are large and ruffled and the quality is excellent. This cultivar has a long bloom period and is distinctive in the garden. *Photo p.10*

'Flames of Fortune' (Peck) Dor 76 cm (30 in) Tet E–M Re Long-time favourite in deep melon tones that absolutely glow. The large flowers are nicely formed and the growth and vigour are excellent. When well established 'Flames of Fortune' will produce an outstanding garden display that literally lights up the garden. *Photo p.36*

'Flower Pavilion' (Kirchoff) Ev 70 cm (28 in) Dip L Re This is a favourite double-flowered daylily. Blooms are large, double and in a clear persimmon-tangerine colour. They are carried in profusion on excellent scapes. This daylily makes a wonderful garden display with a mass of bloom. It is easy growing and one of the very best doubles. *Photo p.24*

'Forever Red' (Kirchoff) Ev 70 cm (28 in) Tet M Re Rich, velvety dark cherry-red with a green throat. Impeccable rounded form, superb branching, lovely ruffling and excellent growth make this a superior daylily. Of all the daylilies I observed in the USA this, as grown in the hybridiser's garden, was the most impressive. It is magnificent in every respect. I now grow it with pride and joy and rate it equally high on performance here in Australia. *Photo p.79*

'Frosted Pink Ice' (Stamile) Dor 70 cm (28 in) Dip E–M Rounded and beautiful ice-pink with a blue influence. The ruffled blooms are held on good scapes but growth is only average and increase is slow. This is strictly one for the connoisseur, but it is a particularly beautiful flower. *Photo p.44*

'Garden Goddess' (Munson) Ev 70 cm (28 in) Tet E–M Re Flowers are large ivory-cream blended melon-yellow with ruffles galore. They are carried in profusion and re-bloom is excellent. 'Garden Goddess' is one of the very best landscaping daylilies for all-round performance.

'Gentle Shepherd' (Yancey) S–Ev to Dor 73 cm (29 in) Dip E–M Re This is the closest to the elusive white. Only a small yellow-green throat adorns the white petals. Substance is only average as is the form but the colour!!! It is really quite pure in its white colouration. *Photo p.20*

'Georgia O'Keefe' (Hansen) S–Ev 60 cm (24 in) Dip M–L Re Buff-melon with a large triangular blue-violet halo and pale lavender edges. Colour and pattern ensure this daylily's popularity. It is unique and was most attractive as seen in the hybridiser's garden.

'Glazed Heather Plum' (Morss) S–Ev 65 cm (26 in) Tet E–M Re Mid purple with a deeper halo, yellow edge and green throat. Full, wide form, well-branched scapes and good growth make this a desirable plant. Although new to my garden it gives every indication of being a quality daylily. *Photo p.20*

'Golden Calypso' (Guidry) Ev 70 cm (28 in) Dip E Re Ruffled golden-orange blended blooms are produced in profusion on excellent scapes. Quality daylily in every respect.

'Grace and Grandeur' (Salter) Ev 63 cm (25 in) Tet E–M Re Round and ruffled pale ivory-cream of very heavy substance. The large flowers are diamond-dusted and repeat bloom is good. This is a special daylily for colour and form. Scapes are well branched and multi-budded. It has proven to be fertile.

'Grand Merci' (Kirchoff) S–Ev 55 cm (22 in) Tet E–M Re Smooth, clear pink with a darker edge. Excellent ruffled form, good scapes and good growth combine to give a very valuable plant in a colour class that is now somewhat overcrowded. This is a lovely flower.

'Grand Palais' (Munson) S–Ev 60 cm (24 in) Tet M Re Flowers are silvery lilac-lavender with a large, round cream throat. They are ruffled and both unusual and attractive. There are now quite a few in this special class but 'Grand Palais' is a pretty flower on a plant that performs well. *Photo p.33*

'Grapes of Wrath' (Kirchoff) Ev 73 cm (29 in) Tet E–M Re Medium-sized clear purple with a deeper area towards the yellow-green throat. Full, rounded and ruffled flowers on quality plants. There are not a lot of high quality purple daylilies but this is a special. *Photo p.20*

'Green Dragon' (Parker) S–Ev 65 cm (26 in) Dip E–M Re Spectacular narrow spider type with narrow curly and recurving petals in green-yellow with a green, radiating throat. This is great on an established clump and gives quite a green effect in the garden. Although the petals are narrow it is not a true 'spider'. It is an excellent landscape daylily. *Photo p.20*

'Green Widow' (Temple) Ev 65 cm (26 in) Dip E Large green-yellow spider with a very green throat giving an overall green effect of true spider flowers. This is one of the best spider daylilies. *Photo p.28*

'Handyman' (Kirchoff) Ev 63 cm (25 in) Dip E–M Re Yellow double with a red eye zone and green throat. Although the flower is attractive this daylily has not been as good for me as it appeared in the hybridiser's garden. It may well improve.

'Happy Hooligan' (Talbott) Ev 45 cm (18 in) Dip E–M Re Cinnamon-red blended double with a green throat. Large, attractive flowers were very attractive in the hybridiser's garden. I have not grown this cultivar. *Photo p.37*

'Eloquent Silence'

'Erica Nicole Gonzales'

Above 'Etosha'

Above left 'Eyed Radiance'

'Extra Strokes'

'Evening Enchantment'

'Fairytale Pink'

Right 'Forever Red'

'Fantasy Quilt'

'Femme Osage'

'High Priestess' (Munson) Ev 105 cm (42 in) Tet M Re Blended bitone of pale pink and rose-pink. Large flowers, good growth and good garden performance make this a long time favourite. It is a tall-growing daylily, well suited to mass display. The flowers have somewhat narrow parts and the form is most distinctive. *Photo p.37*

'Highland Lord' (Munson) S–Ev Tet 55 cm (22 in) Tet M–L Re This wine-red with a lemon-yellow flower is one of the nicest double red daylilies. The medium to large flowers present a garden spectacle at peak bloom. *Photo opposite*

'Holiday in Pink' (Brown) S–Ev 68 cm (27 in) Dip E–M Very ruffled and well-formed cool pink with a green throat. Scapes are well branched and the plant is vigorous. Fertile. *Photo opposite*

'Holy Mackerel' (Kirchoff) Ev 65 cm (26 in) Dip M Re Bright cherry-red double distinctively flecked, edged and striped in pink, yellow and ivory-buff. This is a very unusual double, difficult to obtain and, for me, not quick to multiply. It is, however, a beautiful flower. *Photo opposite*

'Hot Bronze' (Hager) Ev 87 cm (35 in) Tet M Re Blend of red, orange and bronze to give a bronze effect. Large blooms of good form and a plant which performs well. It is an easy grower and prolific bloomer.

'Hot Ember' (Stamile) Ev 76 cm (30 in) Tet M This is a rounded, ruffled and recurved brilliant red-orange flower on a plant of good growth. While attractive in its own right it is in an overcrowded class and much like many others. It is a very fertile cultivar.

'Icy Lemon' (Brooks) S–Ev 85 cm (34 in) Tet E–M Re Very round, ruffled and slightly recurved lemon-yellow with a lime-green throat. Quality of flower, scape and plant is excellent. When better known this will be a much appreciated daylily for its excellent garden performance. It is one of the best lemon-toned daylilies for all-round performance as a specimen or landscape special. *Photo opposite*

'Ida Wimberly Munson' (Munson) S–Ev 70 cm (28 in) Tet M–L Soft lilac-pink of exquisite colouration. Long-time favourite flower with excellent plant performance ensures it a place in the garden although the form has been surpassed in recent years.

'Ida's Magic' (Munson) Ev 70 cm (28 in) Tet E–M Re This large-flowered daylily has created a sensation as one of the first of the heavily ruffled varieties. Colour is peach-pink to amber with a gold edge and green-gold throat. It is deservedly popular, particularly as a breeder for fancy edges. There are many cultivars now available in lines bred from 'Ida's Magic', which is very fertile. *Photo p.82*

'Idle Chatter' (Lee) Ev 55 cm (22 in) Dip E Re Medium-sized white with a red eye zone. Pretty flowers ensure this gives a very attractive garden statement but I have not grown this cultivar. *Photo p.82*

'Inner Peace' (Cratch) Dor 52 cm (21 in) Dip M Re Nicely ruffled and crepe textured, rounded light pink. The small flowers are flat and produced on good scapes. *Photo opposite*

'Iowa Greenery' (Spalding) Ev 50 cm (20 in) Dip E–M Re Rounded and flat green-yellow with a large, intense green throat extending right out to give a very green effect. This provides excellent colour and a well-formed flower. I have not grown this cultivar. *Photo p.10*

'Jalapeno' (Gates) S–Ev 60 cm (24 in) Tet E Re Very large bright maroon-red with a darker eye zone. The attractive blooms are ruffled and of unusual coloration making it a standout in the garden.

'Jamaica Blush' (Kirchoff) Ev 63 cm (25 in) Tet E–M Re Coral-peach blend with a green throat. Large, rounded and ruffled blooms. Beautiful daylily in soft autumn tones. *Photo p.82*

'James Marsh' (Marsh-Klehm) Dor 70 cm (28 in) Tet E–M Very large, nicely formed clear red which is a long-time favourite and remains very popular because of its fine garden performance. This daylily multiplies well and is excellent in colder climates. It often re-blooms for us. *Photo p.83*

'Jean Wootton' (Kirchoff) Ev 70 cm (28 in) Dip E–M Re Nicely formed clear saffron-yellow of beautiful clear colour. This is an excellent daylily for landscaping because of its bold colour statement and excellent garden performance.

'Jedi Codie Wedgeworth' (Wedgeworth) S–Ev 50 cm (20 in) Dip E–M Re Fragrant lavender-pink with a maroon eye zone and green throat. Lovely rounded, ruffled form on a low-growing scape. Flowers are large. *Photo p.83*

'Inner Peace'

Right 'Highland Lord'

Right 'Holiday in Pink'

'Icy Lemon'

'Holy Mackerel'

'Idle Chatter'

'Jamaica Blush'

'Ida's Magic'

'Joan Senior'

'Jennifer Kay O'Neal'

'Jim Jim'

'James Marsh'

'Jedi Codie Wedgeworth'

'Jedi Dot Pierce' (Wedgeworth) S–Ev 50 cm (20 in) Dip E–M Re Fragrant rose-pink bitone with a darker rose-pink eye zone and a green throat. Rounded, ruffled form with large flowers. *Photo p.20*

'Jedi Rose Frost' (Wedgeworth) S–Ev 55 cm (22 in) Dip E Re Large rose-pink with a green throat. This has attractive rounded and ruffled form and is another very nice pink.

'Jennifer Kay O'Neal' (Spalding) Ev 38 cm (15 in) Dip M Re Quality rose-pink of excellent form. Large rounded and ruffled blooms with an unusual texture ensure that this is a standout in the garden. *Photo p.83*

'Jim Jim' (Hansen) S–Ev 55 cm (22 in) Dip M Re Round formed pale creamy yellow double with bands of red. Large attractive blooms are consistently double but, although lovely when viewed individually, the flowers can be sparse on the scape. It is worthy of a place in the garden. *Photo p.83*

'Joan Senior' (Durio) Ev 63 cm (25 in) Dip E–M Re This near white with a lime-green throat has been the most popular daylily we grow and it retains its popularity. The large flowers are carried in profusion on a strong healthy plant. Flower production is superb and the garden display is excellent. It is very close to the elusive white and, when planted in mass, provides a spectacular display over a long period of time. This daylily has passed the test of time and is highly recommended as a specimen plant or for massed display in the landscape. *Photo p.83*

'Jolyene Nichole' (Spalding-Guillory) Ev 35 cm (14 in) Dip M Re Rose-pink blend with deeper rose-pink veining and a green throat. The large flowers are beautifully formed and held well on low scapes. When it is better known this daylily will become very popular. *Photo opposite*

'Jovial' (Gates) Dor 50 cm (20 in) Tet E Re Bright, vivid wine-red with large, ruffled flowers. Quality flowers on quality plants and although dormant, has proven itself in all climates. This is a different shade of red.

'Just Whistle' (Hansen) Ev 65 cm (26 in) Dip E–M Re Ruffled orchid-pink with a dark purple eye and orchid midribs. Beautiful colour and excellent value in the garden, as are so many of this hybridiser's introductions. The colour and pattern of this daylily set it apart from others. *Photo opposite*

'Kelly's Girl' (Spalding) Ev 48 cm (19 in) Dip M Ruffled and recurved coral-rose-pink, slightly bitoned. This is a quality flower and is very popular with landscapers. Although not registered as a rebloomer 'Kelly's Girl' regularly and reliably reblooms for us.

'Kent's Favourite Two' (Kirchoff) Ev 65 cm (26 in) Tet E Re This bright red with a yellow-green throat has been and continues to be very popular. The large flowers are well-formed and produced in profusion on a strong healthy plant. Because of its health, vigour and flower production this ranks as one of the better reds. It is particularly good for massed display and has proven itself to be fertile as a pod and pollen parent. *Photo opposite*

'Kevin Michael Coyne' (Dickerson) Ev 65 cm (26 in) Dip M Re Very large yellow spider with a green throat. This has a long bloom season once established and is one of the better spiders for garden performance. *Photo opposite*

'Kibbutz' (Durio) Ev 65 cm (26 in) Tet E–M Re Large, flat, differently coloured light to rose-pink with ruffles and fluting. Garden habits are good and this is an excellent cultivar for specimen planting as it is a foil for other colours. *Photo opposite*

'Kosciusko' (Unger) Ev 58 cm (23 in) Tet M Re This light greenish yellow has large flowers with a green throat. It is vigorous and prolific and is an outstanding daylily for landscape use because of its health and productivity. 'Kosciusko' is one of the better yellows for massed display. *Photo p.33*

'La Fenice' (Munson) Ev 70 cm (28 in) Tet E–M Re Large, broad and ruffled rose-pink blend. The rounded blooms are striking in the garden and this was most attractive as seen in Florida. I have not grown this daylily.

'La Pêche' (Munson) S–Ev 60 cm (24 in) Tet E–M Re Large peach and yellow blend with a yellow throat. The plant is prolific and the flowers are fragrant. This daylily produces a mass of bloom and is very suitable for landscaping.

'La Rêve' (Hager) Ev 76 cm (30 in) Dip E Re Orchid pink with a green throat. The large blooms are wide with petals overlapping. They are edged in crinkle ruffling. This is a most attractive flower of outstanding quality. Although new it has already proven to be very popular. *Photo p.40*

'Kevin Michael Coyne'

Right 'Kibbutz'

'Jolyene Nichole'

'Kent's Favourite Two'

'Just Whistle'

'Little Isaac'

'Lake Norman Double'

'Lauren Leah'

'Ladybug's Louise'

'Leprechaun's Luck'

'La Scala' (Munson) Ev 76 cm (30 in) Tet M Re Very attractive colour which is a blend of rose-red and cerise with a rosy eye zone. In a clump, this is beautiful and, because of its quick increase, it is easy to obtain a spectacular clump. This is one of the very best daylilies for landscaping and massed display.

'Lady Gail' (Spalding-Guillory) Ev 38 cm (15 in) Dip M Rounded rose-pink with a white edging. Blooms are large and ruffled on a low-growing plant.

'Ladybug's Louise' (Hansen) Ev 55 cm (22 in) Dip M–L Re Smallish flowers are flat, ruffled and mid pink with darker veining and a large rich red eye zone. The flowers are particularly beautiful both as seen in the hybridiser's Florida garden and as grown in Australia. *Photo opposite*

'Lagniappe' (Gates) Ev 50 cm (20 in) Dip E Re Blended coral, peach and pink double of excellent quality. Bloom is plentiful and growth is good. 'Lagniappe' has a most attractive individual bloom of soft delicate colouring.

'Lake Norman Double' (Carpenter) Ev 70 cm (28 in) Dip M Re This is a clear pink double of good quality. The colour is attractive and the bloom is consistently double although the double form often consists of extra petaloids or only three extra petals. *Photo opposite*

'Lauren Leah' (Pierce) S–Ev 50 cm (20 in) Dip E–M Re How many superlatives can one find for a daylily? This soft cream with soft pink highlights has outstanding form, beautiful colour, lovely ruffling and comes on a quality plant of excellent growth and productivity. It is an excellent specimen plant and superb in massed display. I rank 'Lauren Leah' as one of the very best daylilies for any purpose. *Photo opposite*

'Lemon Grass' (Blyth) S–Ev 55 cm (22 in) Tet M Large lemon-yellow of excellent form. The blooms are very ruffled and rounded. This is excellent for massed display and landscaping.

'Lemon Lullaby' (Harris-Benz) Dor 80 cm (32 in) Tet M Re Super quality, full, bright ruffled lemon-yellow. This is a great garden performer. *Photo opposite*

'Lenox' (Munson) Ev 60 cm (24 in) Tet E–M Re Large broad ivory-white of high quality. This is a very floriferous daylily when established and all its garden habits are excellent. The blooms are larger than those of 'Joan Senior' but the plant is less productive. It is, however, a very good all purpose plant.

'Leprechaun's Luck (Kirchoff) Ev 76 cm (30 in) Tet E–M Re This daylily is unique for colour. The large flowers are whisky-orange with a smoky cast. The throat has a butterfly pattern of yellow over a green heart. It has proven to be a colour spectacle in the garden. *Photo opposite*

'Light My Fire' (Kinnebrew) Ev 65 cm (26 in) Dip DM Re Very large gold with a red eye zone. The form is full and the bloom is attractive. This is a good eyed cultivar. *Photo p.88*

'Lin Wright' (Morss) Ev 60 cm (24 in) Tet M Re Alabaster with a wine eye zone and wine edges. Very large blooms are wide and overlapping. This was spectacular as seen in the hybridiser's garden in Florida and it has settled in well in Australia. The petals are wide and diamond-dusted. The well-branched scapes carry many buds and it is very fertile, proving to be an excellent parent for eyed seedlings. *Photo p.88*

'Lines of Splendor' (Temple) Ev 63 cm (25 in) Dip E–M Re Cool yellow spider with a green influence, rose rouging and a red eye zone and green throat. Well-branched classic spider of good growth and garden performance.

'Little Isaac' (Durio) S–Ev 65 cm (26 in) Tet E–M Re This ruffled and frilled hot coral pink blend with deeper pink knobs, edges and fringes is a great personal favourite. Everything about it is top quality and it makes a wonderful display in a clump. I just love the blending of colours and the texture of the blooms. This will be very popular when it is better known. It makes a spectacular colour statement in the garden. *Photo opposite*

'Little Katie' (Durio) Ev 45 cm (18 in) Tet E–M Re Rich deep purple with a darker purple eye zone. The petals are flat and the sepals recurve. Growth and bloom display are excellent. This is one of the better dark purples.

'Lois Hall' (Tarrant) Ev 63 cm (25 in) Dip E–M Re Light lavender and violet-purple with narrow white midribs. Beautiful round, ruffled bitone. Large flowers and good growth ensure the popularity of this very full-flowered daylily. *Photo p.88*

'Lorraine Kilgore' (Munson) S–Ev 76 cm (30 in) Tet M Re This bright pink has been a great favourite. The large bloom is lit up with an apricot throat and has an iridescent sheen. It has good growth and flower production and is very suitable as a specimen plant. *Photo p.88*

'Lemon Lullaby'

Left 'Lois Hall'

Far left 'Lorraine Kilgore'

'Light My Fire'

'Lin Wright'

'Magic Filigree'

'Mariska'

'Mayan Poppy'

'Marilyn Siwik'

'Loving Memories'

'Mask of Time'

Left 'Ming Porcelain'

'Mighty Shogun'

Left 'Midnight Magic'

'Loving Memories' (Spalding) Ev 43 cm (17 in) Dip E Near white self. Large flowers make a low mound of colour. There is little re-bloom but this is very attractive early in the season. *Photo p.89*

'Lyric Opera' (Moldovan) Dor 70 cm (28 in) Tet M Re Quality blooms in an unusual shade of greyed violet-purple are produced on spikes which, in my garden, are much taller than the registered 70 cm (28 in). The blooms are heavily ruffled and have a gold edge. This is a very suitable cultivar for specimen planting at the rear of a garden or border because of its height.

'Magic Filigree' (Salter) Ev 60 cm (24 in) Tet M Re Light lavender with a heavily ruffled golden-yellow edge. This is a spectacular daylily with excellent form and gorgeous colour. I loved it in the hybridiser's garden and have found it a very satisfactory plant to grow. *Photo p.89*

'Majestic Gold' (Guidry) Ev 58 cm (23 in) Dip E Re Very heavily substanced rich gold. The medium-sized, rounded and recurved blooms are most attractive. Garden performance is excellent and this is a distinctive flower in an overcrowded class.

'Mandarin's Coat' (Munson) Ev 63 cm (25 in) Tet E–M Re Rich claret-red with a darker eye. Large, attractive flowers of unusual colour are in bloom for a long period. Although an older cultivar, 'Mandarin's Coat' has not been surpassed in its colour pattern.

'Marble Faun' (Millikan) Ev 72 cm (29 in) Dip E Re This quality daylily is a personal favourite in the cream tones. Unusual lemon marbling is often observed on the large, full, ruffled and fringed blooms. Garden habits are excellent and this is highly recommended.

'Marilyn Siwik' (Kirchoff) Ev 70 cm (28 in) Tet E Re Huge richly coloured orange with a red eye zone and red picotee edge. Wide, flat and ruffled blooms are a colour beacon on good scapes with fine re-bloom. 'Marilyn Siwik' is a new daylily that promises to be one of the best of the very popular eyed cultivars. *Photo p.89*

'Mariska' (Moldovan) Dor 70 cm (28 in) Tet M Re Large, imposing blue-pink flowers undertoned cream are produced on excellent scapes. This daylily is spectacular in a clump and is a very good all-round performer in a range of climates. It is semi-evergreen to evergreen in warmer climates. *Photo p.89*

'Martha Adams' (Spalding) Ev 48 cm (19 in) Dip E–M Re Very ruffled salmon-pink with a green throat and lovely rounded form. This daylily is not a quick increaser but the display of bloom is beautiful. It is a worthy specimen plant.

'Mask of Time' (Salter) S–Ev 63 cm (25 in) Tet M Re Bright coral-rose with a black-purple eye and black-purple picotee edge. The colour is sensational and the large flowers a spectacle when in bloom. This is very suitable for specimen planting. *Photo opposite*

'Mayan Poppy' (Munson) Ev 60 cm (24 in) Tet M Re Multicoloured blend in sunset colours of coral, pink and amber. Beautiful round and ruffled blooms on excellent plants make this a great favourite. It is the potpourri of colour which sets this daylily apart. *Photo p.89*

'Midnight Magic' (Kinnebrew) Ev 70 cm (28 in) Tet E–M Re Very dark red near-black with a green throat. This often grows tall and the prolific blooming habits present a colour spectacle. One of the very best and most popular daylilies for massed display where a tall, dark cultivar is required. 'Midnight Magic' has proven to be an excellent parent. *Photo opposite*

'Mighty Shogun' (Moldovan) S–Ev 65 cm (26 in) Tet E–M Re Ruffled, velvety, rich deep burgundy-maroon self of large size and good quality. This daylily provides excellent contrast with the lighter colours and is a very good grower. *Photo opposite*

'Ming Porcelain' (Kirchoff) Ev 70 cm (28 in) Tet E Re Ivory-pink with a gold edge, yellow halo and lime-green throat. This is a beautiful and prolific daylily with outstanding garden habits and the porcelain finish sets it apart from other cultivars. *Photo opposite*

'Ming Temple' (Munson) S–Ev 65 cm (26 in) Tet E–M Re This is a prolifically blooming daylily with large flowers in tones of cream to melon. Because of its long bloom season it is excellent for landscaping. *Photo p.92*

'Misha' (Peck) Dor 65 cm (26 in) Tet M Medium-sized flowers are bright red with a green throat. This daylily is an easy grower and is excellent in a clump. The colour is very bright and distinctive.

'Missouri Memories' (Hansen) Ev 65 cm (26 in) Dip M–L Re Soft, pale creamy pink-lavender with a deeper pink band, chartreuse throat and diamond dusting. This is one of the loveliest daylilies I saw in the USA—spectacular in Florida and it is superb in Australia. The colour pattern is soft and subdued. This is a great specimen plant. *Photo p.92*

Above 'Ming Temple'

Left 'Missouri Memories'

'Monica Mead'

'Morocco'

'Monica Marie'

Right 'Moonlit Masquerade'

'Monrovia Gem'

'Mokan Butterfly' (Lenington) S–Ev 87 cm (35 in) Tet E–M Re Near white with a bold lavender halo and edge. The large ruffled flowers are produced in profusion and present a stunning display in a clump. This daylily is extremely popular and deservedly so. As a clump it attracts more attention than any other daylily at the nursery so this is a fair measure of its impact. Superb daylily. *Photo p.10*

'Molino Pink Loveliness' (McCord) Ev 45 cm (18 in) Dip E Re Pastel pink of lovely colour set off with a rose-pink halo and chartreuse throat. The flowers are of beautiful form with exquisite ruffling. I have not grown this beauty.

'Monica Marie' (Gates) S–Ev to Dor 60 cm (24 in) E Re This is one of the loveliest of the white daylilies with well-formed, rounded and ruffled blooms. It is spectacular in bloom but has not been a quick increaser for me. *Photo p.93*

'Monica Mead' (Kirchoff) Ev 50 cm (20 in) Dip E Re Very attractive light pink double of attractive form and consistent bloom. Nice branching and bud count and good re-bloom. This promises to be one of the best doubles. *Photo p.92*

'Monrovia Gem' (Hankinson) Ev 80 cm (32 in) Tet E–M Re This light to mid orange with a darker re-bloom has been a delight to grow. The large flowers are produced in profusion over a long bloom period and this is one of the best landscaping daylilies because of its superb growth. It is healthy, vigorous and prolific and is very highly recommended where health, vigour and productivity are essential. *Photo p.93*

'Moon Snow' (Munson) S–Ev 60 cm (24 in) Tet E–M Re Large, very ruffled ivory-white of good form. This is a quality near white which grows well.

'Moon Twilight' (Munson) S–Ev 55 cm (22 in) Tet E–M Re Lovely bright but light pink of excellent quality. The flowers are large, broad and circular and growth is excellent. Everything about this daylily is top quality and it is deservedly popular. *Photo p.6*

'Moonlit Masquerade' (Salter) S–Ev 70 cm (28 in) Tet E–M–L Re Clear white with a dark purple eye and edge and a dark green throat. Quality daylily with an extended bloom season. *Photo p.93*

'Moroccan Summer' (Kirchoff) Ev 55 cm (22 in) Dip E–M Re This intense, rich gold double is very symmetrical and of very good quality. I have not been able to observe this daylily as a clump but it has shown promise. *Photo p.96*

'Morocco' (Harris-Benz) Dor 76 cm (30 in) Tet M Re Blend of bronze and rosy orange giving a pastel bronze effect. Lovely large, well-rounded and ruffled blooms in a colour that has not proven popular but is attractive. *Photo p.92*

'Most Noble' (Munson) Ev 70 cm (28 in) Tet M Re Large, fluted lemon-yellow blooms are produced in abundance on excellent scapes. This is a high quality daylily, very suitable for landscape use or specimen planting.

'Nagasaki' (Kirchoff) Ev 50 cm (20 in) Dip E–M Re Medium-sized double flowers are a pastel blend of ivory, cream, pink and lavender and are produced in abundance. The blooms are ruffled and the quality is good. Although an older cultivar 'Nagasaki' retains its popularity. *Photo opposite*

'Nairobi Night' (Munson) S–Ev 76 cm (30 in) Tet M Re Plum-violet with a large light eye pattern of ivory overlaid lavender. The large flowers are broad, flat, rounded and ruffled. It is very popular because of its unusual and attractive colour. *Photo p.96*

'Nanuq' (Jinkerson) Dor 68 cm (27 in) Dip M–L Medium-sized, near white flowers on an easy growing plant. Flower substance is good and this is a worthwhile addition to the near whites.

'Navajo Princess' (Hansen) Dor 60 cm (24 in) Dip M–L Re Mid pink with a rose-pink eye zone, chartreuse throat and green heart. Medium-sized flowers are diamond-dusted. This is a very pretty and different daylily; I have not observed this colour pattern previously. The garden effect is soft and delicate. *Photo opposite*

'Nebuchadnezzar's Furnace' (Talbott) Ev 55 cm (22 in) Dip M Re Unusual shade of red flowers, very double and very consistent. The blooms are large and this is worth a place in the garden for its interesting and different colour. It presents a great splash of colour when in bloom. *Photo opposite*

'Niece Beverly' (Spalding-Guillory) Dor 38 cm (19 in) Dip M Ruffled, ribbed and veined lavender with a deeper lavender eye zone and white midribs. This makes a pretty low mound of colour. *Photo p.96*

'Night Wings' (Williams) Ev 76 cm (30 in) Tet E Re Very dark red-black with a green throat and a velvet sheen. Large flowers are a beacon in the garden and the tall scapes ensure this is a standout. It is beautiful when planted with soft creams to give great contrast. *Photo opposite*

'Night Wings'

Right 'Navajo Princess'

'Nebuchadnezzar's Furnace'

'Nagasaki'

'Nile Plum'

Left 'Moroccan Summer'

'Old Tangiers'

'Nuance'

'Nairobi Night'

'Niece Beverly'

'Paper Butterfly'

Left 'Palace Guard'

'Ocean Rain'

'Paiges Pinata'

'Panache'

'Our Kirsten'

'Oriental Dancer'

'Oriental Opulence'

'Panchen Lama'

'Nile Plum' (Munson) Ev 50 cm (20 in) Tet E–M Re A large creamy eye extends way out into this rich plum-violet giving sharp contrast. The large flowers are carried on healthy plants and the colour pattern is most unusual with the blending and contrasting of colours. This daylily has proven very popular and is fertile. *Photo p.96*

'Nivia Guest' (Munson) Ev 60 cm (24 in) Tet M Re Purple with a green-yellow throat. Large, ruffled flowers on a very good plant. It is an unusual shade of purple.

'Nuance' (Gates) Ev 50 cm (20 in) Dip E Re Large, ruffled and very nicely formed cream with a green throat. This is a special daylily, elegant yet robust. It is a personal favourite because of its classic sculptured appearance and is an excellent specimen plant. *Photo p.96*

'Ocean Rain' (Hanson) S–Ev 65 cm (26 in) Tet E–M Beautiful, broad, rounded clear lavender-orchid rimmed in gold. Large flowers are produced in profusion on healthy plants. This is a subtle but beautiful flower and a great personal favourite. It is very popular. *Photo p.97*

'Old Tangiers' (Millikan) S–Ev 70 cm (28 in) Tet M–L Re Quality red-orange that is an excellent performer. Large, wide and ruffled flowers are a beacon in the garden, and it is very productive. *Photo p.96*

'Olive Bailey Langdon' (Munson) Ev 70 cm (28 in) Tet VE-VL Re Deep violet-purple, lightly ruffled with a yellow-green throat. This is a quality daylily with excellent garden habits and prolific bloom. It is a long-time favourite and retains its popularity. Because of its all-round performance it is recommended for mass planting.

'Oriental Dancer' (Brown) S–Ev 68 cm (27 in) Tet E–M Pink, cream and yellow blend with a yellow throat and green heart bordered by a subtle rose-pink halo. Blooms are wide, ruffled, full formed and rolled back. This daylily is unique for form and colour and although new to this country has attracted much attention. It will be very popular when established. *Photo opposite*

'Oriental Opulence' (Salter) S–Ev 75 cm (30 in) Tet E–M Re Cream and yellow blend with pink highlights and a large green throat. Beautiful large, round and heavily ruffled flowers. Excellent quality bloom and plant ensure popularity once this new variety is established. Fertile. *Photo opposite*

'Our Kirsten' (Hansen) Ev 65 cm (26 in) Dip E–M–L Re Flat, diamond-dusted, ruffled peach-pink of good substance on a well-branched scape. This daylily produces masses of bloom over an extended period. Fertile. *Photo opposite*

'Outrageous' (Stevens) Dor 55 cm (22 in) Tet M–L Light burnt orange with a large mahogany-red eye zone. Stunning bloom but growth and increase are below average for us. It is the spectacular colour pattern which sets this daylily apart. It may be a better performer in really cold climates. *Photo p.48*

'Over The Edge' (Salter) S–Ev 60 cm (24 in) Tet M Re Super ruffled large lavender-rose with a gold edge. Sensational daylily as seen in the hybridiser's garden but I have not grown it.

'Paiges Pinata' (Hansen) S–Ev 65 cm (26 in) Dip E–M Re Peach-pink with a fuchsia-pink band and large orange-pink eye zone and green throat. Ruffled flowers are large and unusual and soft in colouration yet rich and spectacular. I loved this daylily as seen in Florida and can only hope it performs as well in Australia, where it has settled in well. *Photo opposite*

'Palace Guard' (Munson) S–Ev 70 cm (28 in) Tet M–L Re Very bright red with a satin sheen. Large flowers are produced in quantity and the growth is good. This is a long-time favourite bright red, very suitable for massed display. *Photo p.97*

'Pam Sims' (Oxley) Dor 65 cm (26 in) Tet M–L Very ruffled soft apricot which is slow opening but very beautiful in hot weather with warm nights. When it is good it is very good but it does not like cold nights.

'Panache' (Munson) Ev 70 cm (28 in) Tet M–L Re Cream with a purple eye and purple picotee edge. The large flowers are produced in profusion and this is one of the first of the exciting new range of picotees. Lovely! 'Panache' has excellent garden habits. *Photo opposite*

'Panchen Lama' (Munson) S–Ev 70 cm (28 in) Tet M Re Large smooth ivory-cream-pink with a precise rose-pink eye zone. This is a very attractive pastel that grows and flowers well. *Photo opposite*

'Paper Butterfly' (Morss) S–Ev 60 cm (24 in) Tet E–L Re Peach with a blue-violet eye zone and green throat. Large flowers, unusual form but attractive in the garden where it is quite distinctive. *Photo p.97*

'Pink Charming'

Right 'Passionate Prize'

'Pastel Classic'

'Passionate Prize' (Brown) Ev 65 cm (26 in) Tet E–M Re Large smooth rose-pink blend with a white petal stripe. Distinctive, attractive, healthy and vigorous, this daylily is suitable for specimen planting or massed display. *Photo opposite*

'Pastel Classic' (Millikan) S–Ev 58 cm (23 in) Dip M Re This daylily is well named. It is a most beautiful, ruffled pink, pale and delicate. The large flowers are rounded and very ruffled. Growth habits are good. This is a personal favourite and a daylily of outstanding merit. It ranks very highly as an all-round performer. One of the best! *Photo opposite*

'Pat Mercer' (Joiner) S–Ev 70 cm (28 in) Dip M This daylily lasts longer than a day. It opens a bright orange-red and on the second day is a rich dark orange. The plant is robust and the 'two-day' flower a bonus. *Photo p. 103*

'Pearl Hammond' (Tarrant) Ev 68 cm (27 in) Dip E–M Re Ruffled rose-pink with a darker midrib and a chartreuse-green throat. This daylily is very attractive in a class with many cultivars deserving attention.

'Pearl Lewis' (Peck) Dor 60 cm (24 in) Tet M–L Re Ruffled pure gold of outstanding quality. The very large flowers are of excellent form and come on quality scapes from strong plants. This daylily is highly recommended for colder climates.

'Perfect Pie' (Kirchoff) S–Ev 58 cm (23 in) Tet E–M Re Medium-sized flowers are bright lemon-yellow with ornate filigree-laced edges. Form is rounded and very ruffled. Blooms very well as seen in the hybridiser's garden and it has settled in well in Australia.

'Persistent Memories' (Stamile) S–Ev 68 cm (27 in) Dip E–M Blue-pink of very nice colouring. Large, well-branched and heavily ruffled. I have not yet seen this cultivar on an established clump in its Australian garden.

'Phoenecian Ruffles' (Stamile) S–Ev 63 cm (25 in) Tet E–M Re Large, fluted and ruffled clear grape-purple with a deeper eye zone. Bloom is prolific on multi-budded scapes and the flower colour is distinctive. Its major appeal is the heavy ruffling on the flowers.

'Pink Charming' (Brown) S–Ev 65 cm (26 in) Dip E–M Rounded and recurved clear pink. Exquisite form and lovely colour make this a most attractive daylily. It has settled in well but has not yet developed into a clump for us. *Photo opposite*

'Pink For Two' (Kirchoff) Ev 50 cm (20 in) Dip M Medium-sized double pink with a rose-pink halo and green throat. The attractive blooms are wide and ruffled and this daylily is a real showoff. It was beautiful as seen in Florida and should be a top quality acquisition.

'Pink Gloss' (Pierce) S–Ev 50 cm (20 in) Dip E–M Re Large, well-formed pink with a green throat. Form is wide, rounded and ruffled and the flower is most attractive.

'Pink Pompon' (Stamile) Ev 55 cm (22 in) Tet E–M Re Rich coral-pink blended double with excellent garden performance. The blooms have a glow that sets them apart and flowers are consistently double. This daylily is highly recommended. *Photo p. 102*

'Pink Tranquility' (Brown) Ev 75 cm (30 in) Dip E–M Re Beautiful pink with a green throat. Large, ruffled flowers are rounded and of outstanding form to give a gorgeous effect in the garden. This is a quality new daylily. *Photo p. 102*

'Pirate's Patch' (Salter) Ev 70 cm (28 in) Tet M–L Re Cream with a plum-black eye and edge. This large flowered daylily is stunning in the garden and is an excellent grower. The sharp contrast between the base colour and the eye sets this flower apart. The well-branched scapes are multi-budded and the plant is fertile. *Photo p. 104*

'Pocket of Dreams' (Gates) S–Ev 45 cm (18 in) Dip E–M Re Creamy pink blending to darker pink edges. Large ruffled flowers of excellent substance and plants that grow with ease make this a desirable daylily.

'Porcelain Finery' (Pierce-Wilson) S–Ev 45 cm (18 in) Dip E–M Re Ruffled and flat ivory blend of perfectly rounded form. The porcelain finish adds to the beauty of these exquisite flowers. *Photo p. 102*

'Porcelain Prince' (Munson) Ev 90 cm (36 in) Tet E–M Re Very nice and different yellow with pastel pink rouging. The large flowers are fluted, produced in profusion and attractive in the garden.

'Precious Princess' (Moldovan) S–Ev 70 cm (28 in) Tet M Re Large flowered ivory with a porcelain finish. Attractive ruffled blooms are very delicate in appearance. I love the porcelain-like texture. *Photo p. 102*

'Prime Minister' (Munson) Dor 76 cm (30 in) Tet M Re Full-formed brilliant orange-red of exciting colour. The large flowers are ruffled, most attractive and freely produced. The colour is a standout in the garden.

Above 'Precious Princess'

Above left 'Porcelain Finery'

Opposite 'Pat Mercer'

'Pink Tranquility'

'Pink Pompon'

Right 'Purple Storm'

'Proud Mary'

'Proud Princess'

'Pirate's Patch'

'Pure and Simple'

'Pumpkin Kid'

'Raging Tiger'

Right 'Razzle'

Below 'Radiant Ruffles'

Below right 'Queen Lily'

'Quick Results'

'Raspberry Wine'

'Rachel My Love'

'Pushmataha'

'Quietness'

'Priscilla's Rainbow' (Spalding-Guillory) Dor 55 cm (22 in) Dip M Very large and round pink-lavender blend with a rainbow halo. Attractive, colourful ruffled blooms are most unusual, subdued and excitingly different.

'Proud Mary' (Salter) Ev 65 cm (26 in) Tet M–L Re Mid pink with a yellow-green throat. Form is rounded, wide and ruffled while the flowers are large and most attractive. This is a special daylily which was outstanding in the hybridiser's garden in Florida and has settled in very well in Australia. It is vigorous and fertile. *Photo p. 104*

'Proud Princess' (Kirchoff) S–Ev 70 cm (28 in) Tet E Re Rose-pink bitone with a greyed rose halo and a green throat. Wide, overlapping blooms and consistent bloom make this a good daylily. *Photo p. 104*

'Pumpkin Kid' (Spalding) Ev 45 cm (18 in) Dip M Re Orange with a red eye and green throat. The large ruffled blooms are spectacular in the garden with a great display of colour. This is a special daylily with high appeal because of its colour pattern and clarity of colour. *Photo p. 104*

'Pure and Simple' (Salter) S–Ev 70 cm (28 in) Tet E–M Re Orange-sherbet with an olive-green throat. This is an outstanding daylily of rounded ruffled form and excellent colouration. It is very special, as seen in Florida, and has already proven itself in Australia. Excellent scapes carry multiple blooms. Fertile. *Photo p. 104*

'Purple Rain Dance' (Brown) Ev 73 cm (29 in) Dip E–M Re Deep purple with a green throat. Vigorous plant habits ensure that this will be a top quality purple once it is established.

'Purple Storm' (Webster) S–Ev 65 cm (26 in) Tet M Unusual, attractive and very showy pink-lavender with a purple edge and large deep purple eye. It is the colour pattern which sets this apart from others in the class. *Photo p. 102*

'Pushmataha' (Gates) Ev 60 cm (24 in) Tet E Re Very large bright red with a chartreuse throat. The rounded, ruffled blooms are of excellent form and different colouring. This is special because of the unique shading of colouration, the quality of the flower and the garden habits. It will not be mistaken for any other daylily. *Photo opposite*

'Queen Empress' (Munson) Ev 70 cm (28 in) Tet E–M Re Delicately ruffled flesh-pink shaded ivory-yellow and pink. The fragrant blooms are large, flat and rounded. Growth and production are excellent.

'Queen Lily' (Kirchoff) Ev 60 cm (24 in) Dip E–M Re Double flowers in a cream-pink blend with a green throat. Nice flowers with consistent double bloom but the flowers are only lightly double. *Photo p. 105*

'Quick Results' (Brooks) S–Ev to Ev 83 cm (33 in) Tet E–M Re This is a favourite bright yellow daylily. The very large, beautifully formed and ruffled flowers have a green throat and are produced in profusion over a long period. Health, vigour, growth and quality of scape are excellent. This is a landscape delight. It is certainly my favourite yellow and among the very top few of all the daylilies I have grown. If I could grow only one daylily, this would have to be *the* one! *Photo opposite*

'Quietness' (Spalding) S–Ev 48 cm (19 in) Dip E–M Re Very large cream with a pink influence and a green throat. This is a daylily of outstanding form and is one of the loveliest in the garden. Outstanding in every way, 'Quietness' is so popular we can never keep up the demand. *Photo opposite*

'Rachel My Love' (Talbott) Ev 45 cm (18 in) Dip E–M Re Yellow double with a green throat. Superb quality large flowers. Prolific bloom and very vigorous growth make this one of the great daylilies. There is little to choose between 'Betty Woods' and 'Rachel My Love' as the best yellow double. *Photo opposite*

'Radiant Ruffles' (Brown) Ev 60 cm (24 in) Dip M–L Re Small to medium flowers are cream with a rich red eye, gold throat and olive heart. Superb ruffled, rounded form, prolific bloom and great growth make this one of the very best performers for those who are happy with a smaller sized flower. It is very highly recommended. *Photo p. 105*

'Raging Tiger' (Rasmussen) Dor 63 cm (25 in) Tet M Fantastic bright burnt orange with a shocking large wine-red eye zone. This daylily is stunning in a clump and is excellent for colder climates. It has proven to be very popular. *Photo p. 105*

'Raspberry Wine' (Wild) Dor 50 cm (20 in) Dip L Late flowering raspberry-red with well-formed and unusually textured blooms. This is an older variety, still worthy because of the textured flower form. *Photo opposite*

'Razzle' (Hansen) Ev 70 cm (28 in) Dip M–L Ruffled dark violet small flower with a bold purple eye zone. Grow it with 'Dazzle' and have a 'razzle-dazzle'. This is a very nice, smaller-flowered, eyed cultivar. *Photo p. 105*

'Roses with Peaches'

'Rose Emily'

'Royal Heiress'

'Romantic Dreams'

'Rose Frilly Dilly'

'Reba My Love' (Talbott) Ev 70 cm (28 in) Dip E–M Re Pearly shell-pink double flowers are large and full formed. Excellent branching, many buds and quality growth make this a top quality daylily. In my experience, it has been consistently double once established and is one of the most beautiful daylilies.

'Rebecca Sue Memorial' (Spalding) Ev 58 cm (23 in) Dip E–M This is my favourite daylily from this talented hybridiser. The large blooms are a delicate soft pink with glistening pearl highlights. They are round, ruffled and perfectly formed. One of the best pastels for all-round performance and this daylily has re-bloomed for us. It is highly recommended and is one of the top few daylilies available. *Photo p. 110*

'Regal Tapestry' (Munson) Ev 76 cm (30 in) Tet M Re Large creamy gold with wide burgundy chevrons. This older daylily still holds much appeal for its colour pattern which is unusual and attractive. Plant habits and general performance are good.

'Renaissance Fair' (Munson) Ev 70 cm (28 in) Tet M Re Smooth silvery mauve with a dark burgundy-purple eye. Large, nicely formed blooms are very eye-catching and this daylily holds much appeal.

'Respighi' (Munson) Ev 50 cm (20 in) Tet E–M Re Wine-purple with a chalky wine eye zone and a yellow-green throat. Unusual and attractive colour but it has not proven very vigorous in my garden. It is fertile.

'Riptide' (Millikan) Ev 55 cm (22 in) Dip E–M Quality, flat, recurved lemon-yellow with ruffles. This is a very pretty flower on a plant which performs well.

'Riseman's Flame' (Hansen) S–Ev 60 cm (24 in) Dip E–M–L Re Lightly ruffled yellow with a rose-red pattern on the outer parts of the flower and a small green throat. Large flowers on a long-blooming plant. This is a daylily which performs very well. *Photo p. 110*

'Romantic Dreams' (Stamile) S–Ev 58 cm (23 in) Tet E–M Re Deep lavender-pink 12 cm (5 in) blooms with large green throat and deep ruffling are heavily substanced. Well-branched and multi-budded scapes. *Photo opposite*

'Rose Cherub' (Spalding) S–Ev 48 cm (19 in) Dip M Large, well formed rose-red of excellent form. General performance is very satisfactory.

'Rose Emily' (Pierce) Dor to S–Ev 45 cm (18 in) Dip M Re Rose-pink with a very green throat. Beautiful ruffled flowers are amongst the loveliest of all daylilies. Highly recommended to those who love pink flowers, particularly when highlighted by the green in the throat. This is not quick to increase but is very satisfying to grow. *Photo opposite*

'Rose Frilly Dilly '(Gleber) Dor 65 cm (26 in) Dip E–M Re Large heavily ruffled rose-pink with a slightly deeper eye zone. This daylily is multi-budded and has a long bloom season. The floral parts are somewhat narrow but the heavy ruffling adds to its beauty. *Photo opposite*

'Rose Joy' (Carpenter) Dor 55 cm (22 in) Dip M Re Large strawberry-rose with an eye zone of creamy white and green. This is a lovely flower accented by particularly beautiful new foliage in spring. It is one of the best dormant cultivars and the hosta-like foliage in spring is an added bonus. *Photo p. 110*

'Rose Talisman' (Harris-Benz) Dor 76 cm (30 in) Tet E–M Large and imposing circular deep rose with a coral to orange influence. The colour of this daylily is very variable in different soil conditions and I have seen it looking quite pink and in other gardens very much in orange tonings.

'Rose Tattoo' (Moldovan) Dor 65 cm (26 in) Tet E Re Unusual rose-pink with a ruffled white picotee edge and midrib. Large flowers are unique for colour and pattern and the plant habits are good. *Photo p. 110*

'Roses with Peaches' (Kirchoff) S–Ev 55 cm (22 in) Tet E–M Re Small to medium-sized peach-pink with a rose-pink eye zone and yellow-green throat. This new variety is very rounded and nicely ruffled. It has a gorgeous colour pattern and is very quick to repeat bloom. *Photo opposite*

'Royal Dancer' (Sikes) Ev 63 cm (25 in) Tet M Re Very attractive brick-red with a faint deeper halo. This well ruffled, large flower is top quality and is a great favourite. This is distinctly different in the red tones.

'Royal Heiress '(Munson) Ev 60 cm (24 in) Tet E–M Re Super quality, bold rich plum-burgundy with a chalky circular eye. The large ruffled flowers are carried on excellent scapes and the growth and increase are top quality. This is a great daylily in the garden although the colour is subdued rather than vibrant. *Photo opposite*

'Rose Joy'

Right 'Rebecca Sue Memorial'

'Riseman's Flame'

'Rose Tattoo'

'Ruby Sullivan'

Above right 'Silken Touch'

Right 'Ruffled Perfection'

'Ruffled Shawl'

Above 'Scarlet Orbit'

Left 'Ruffles Elegante'

'Seminole Wind'

'Serena Dark Horse'

'Seminole Dream'

'Royal Legacy' (Munson) S–Ev 60 cm (24 in) Tet M–L Re Large, rounded and ruffled lemon-yellow makes a beautiful display in the garden or in the landscape where a soft but clear yellow on low-growing scapes is required.

'Royal Prestige' (Hite) Dor 70 cm (28 in) Tet M–L Very large rich blue-purple with white edges. Distinctive blooms are most attractive. This is an excellent daylily for colder climates. *Photo p.11*

'Royal Trumpeter' (Munson) Dor 76 cm (30 in) Tet M–L Brilliant orange-red with a deeper red eye. The large blooms are most colourful and a beacon in the garden. Although dormant, 'Royal Trumpeter' has proven to be very popular.

'Ruby Sullivan' (Brown) S–Ev 60 cm (24 in) Dip VE Re Bright pink with a darker pink halo and wide green throat. Quality flower and it has settled in well to Australian conditions. *Photo p.111*

'Ruffled Ballet' (Harris-Benz) Dor 76 cm (30 in) Tet M This is the nicest yellow that I have grown but alas it is slow to increase. Super quality round ruffled blooms are pure yellow. Scapes are excellent and the plant is healthy. Outstanding in a clump or as an individual flower. 'Ruffled Ballet' is recommended as the best available dormant yellow if you have a little patience. *Photo p.40*

'Ruffled Double Frills' (Brown) S–Ev 60 cm (24 in) Dip E–M Re Very attractive double lemon-yellow with a green throat. The large flowers are consistently double and it is worthy of a place in the garden.

'Ruffled Feathers' (Peck) Dor 65 cm (26 in) Tet M Re Very fine quality pink with excellent garden performance. This dormant pink is suitable for colder climates.

'Ruffled Ivory' (Brown) S–Ev 65 cm (26 in) Dip M Re Ivory to white with a chartreuse throat. Beautiful large ruffled flowers of exquisite form, the trademark of this hybridiser.

'Ruffled Magic' (Brown) Ev 63 cm (25 in) Dip E–M Light yellow with a pink blush and undertone. Lovely large ruffled flowers of beautiful colouration and excellent form but, unfortunately, it has not proven a heavy bloomer.

'Ruffled Perfection' (Carpenter) Ev 60 cm (24 in) Dip E Re Fragrant lemon-yellow with a green throat. Beautiful, large blooms—gorgeous at every stage. This is a top quality daylily with heavily ruffled flowers. *Photo p.111*

'Ruffled Shawl' (Spalding) S–Ev 30 cm (12 in) Dip M Very large flowers on a very low-growing plant present a carpet of colour in rich pink with darker veins and halo. Quality is superb in every respect and we have had consistent re-bloom from this daylily. It is recommended as a low-growing specimen or for massed display and is very satisfactory for pot culture. *Photo p.111*

'Ruffles Elegante' (Munson) S–Ev 80 cm (32 in) Tet M–L Re Fluted and ruffled orchid-rose-pink with a large watermarked centre in creamy pink. The large flowers and prolific bloom make this a garden spectacle over a long period in the season. *Photo p.112*

'Sachet of Lemon' (Kirchoff) Ev 65 cm (26 in) Dip E Re Mid yellow with darker edges and a green throat. Unique colouring sets this daylily apart and the flowers are pleated and ruffled. Great quality for bloom and growth. 'Sachet of Lemon' is an excellent landscape daylily.

'Sanford House' (Kirchoff) S–Ev 65 cm (26 in) Dip E Re Medium-sized rose-pink double. Prolific bloom although the pink tone is somewhat dull compared to more recent releases and this daylily is useful as an accent to brighter colours.

'Sariah' (Gage) S–Ev 48 cm (19 in) Dip E Re Round and ruffled clear melon-pink with wax-like substance and beautiful form. Excellent daylily with very good garden performance.

'Sarsaparilla' (Gates) Ev 70 cm (28 in) Tet E Re Very large apricot with a green throat. The plant is vigorous and prolific and this ranks with 'Simply Pretty' as the best of the rich apricots for massed display.

'Save the Children' (Hansen) Ev 65 cm (26 in) Dip M–L Re Pink and cream bicolour of fancy colouration. The cream sepals have pink edges and the pink petals have cream edges. Unusual and attractive colouration will ensure great popularity for this daylily.

'Scarlet Orbit' (Gates) Ev 55 cm (22 in) Tet E Re Lightly fragrant bright scarlet-red with a slightly darker halo and green throat. Superb quality, large ruffled flowers. Prolific bloom and outstanding plant habits make this one of the very best of all. It is certainly the best landscaping red and a large planting is a sight to be seen. This daylily is recommended for those who want a long flowering, bright red of great colour and excellent performance on a low-growing plant. *Photo p.112*

'Scarlock' (Peck) Dor 76 cm (30 in) Tet E–M Re This long-time favourite is a dark red with a green throat. The large imposing blooms are outstanding. This is one of the best of the dormant reds and is excellent in colder climates.

'Second Glance' (Sellers) Dor S–Ev 70 cm (28 in) Tet M–L Nicely ruffled large flowers are bright tangerine-persimmon. The plant is a prolific producer of quality flowers. 'Second Glance' ranks with 'Simply Pretty' and 'Sarsaparilla' for tops in the orange-apricot tones.

'Secret Splendor' (Salter) Ev 63 cm (25 in) Tet M–L Re Light lavender-rose with a yellow-green throat. Large, attractive, ruffled flowers on good plants as seen in Florida. This daylily has already settled in well to Australian conditions and will be popular. *Photo p.41*

'Seductor' (Gates) Ev 45 cm (18 in) Tet E Re Fragrant red with a green throat. Large ruffled flowers of excellent form on a quality plant but bloom is not as prolific as 'Scarlet Orbit'.

'Seminole Dream' (Kirchoff) Ev 45 cm (18 in) Dip E–M Re Lemon-yellow double with a green throat. Rounded, full form and plentiful bloom of medium-sized flowers. This was gorgeous as seen in Florida and I am hopeful that it will be equally as good in Australia. Initial performance indicates that will be so. *Photo p.113*

'Seminole Wind' (Stamile) Ev 58 cm (23 in) Tet E–M Re This just could be the nicest pink daylily! Rich clear pink with an olive-green throat. Large, rounded and ruffled flowers of perfect form and good growth make this an excellent cultivar. It was superb as seen in the hybridiser's garden in Florida. Initial bloom in Australia was sensational and this will rank as one of the best once established. Scapes are well-branched and it is very fertile, producing outstanding seedlings. *Photo p.113*

'Semiramide' (Munson) Dor 70 cm (28 in) Tet E–M Wine-red with a chalky eye zone. Very attractive large flowers but bloom production and growth have not proven to be good.

'Serena Dark Horse' (Marshall-Benz) Dor 88 cm (35 in) Tet E–M Tall-growing dark red-black with a green throat. The large imposing flowers are a great contrast for lighter colours and are attractive in their own right. This ranks with 'Midnight Magic' as the best of the tall, dark, daylilies and it is excellent for planting at the back of a display. *Photo p.113*

'Shaman' (Gates) Ev 50 cm (20 in) Tet E Re Super quality green-yellow with a green throat. This daylily abounds with quality! Large ruffled flowers and excellent growth place this at a very high level in a very crowded class. 'Shaman' has proven very popular.

'Shaolin Priest' (Woodhall) S–Ev 60 cm (24 in) Tet M Re This is a most attractive blend of creamy coral undercast with salmon-rose accented by a ruffled golden filigree edge and a large golden-amber sunburst watermark. It is a sensational flower on a great plant and, seen in a mass planting is an eyecatcher. It is highly recommended. *Photo p.17*

'Shinto Etching' (Munson) Ev 65 cm (26 in) Tet E–M Re Very attractive pastel mauve-ivory bitone. Very large flowers of attractive ruffled form. Good quality flowers but I cannot report on its growth and vigour. It is fertile. *Photo p.17*

'Shirred Lace' (Wilson) S–Ev 45 cm (18 in) Dip E–M Re Ruffled bright yellow with great clarity of colour. The lacy flowers are medium-sized and distinctively different because of this lace. I have only grown this daylily for a short period but it is very promising. *Photo p.40*

'Shockwave' (Brown) S–Ev 76 cm (30 in) Tet E Re Very large golden-yellow flowers are produced in profusion throughout the season. The ruffled blooms are of excellent quality and the scapes are tall and imposing. This is an excellent landscaping subject.

'Sight Delight' (Gates) Ev 60 cm (24 in) Dip E Re This dark rosy pink with a rosy red eye zone and lighter edge has an exciting colour combination to ensure popularity. Growth, vigour and garden habits are excellent. 'Sight Delight' is among the very best dark pink cultivars for mass display.

'Silent Sentry' (Salter) S–Ev 60 cm (24 in) Tet E–M Very unusual purple self with large patterned ivory-yellow-green throat. This is a distinctive daylily and most attractive in the garden. It was particularly beautiful as seen in Florida but has taken time to settle into Australian conditions. It has heavy substance and well-branched scapes. It is fertile.

'Silken Touch' (Stamile) S–Ev 58 cm (23 in) Tet E–M Re Bright rose-pink of very good quality. Form is rounded and ruffled and plant habits from initial experience are very good. It has heavy substance, excellent form and is very fertile. *Photo p.111*

'Timeless Fire'

Above 'Sorcerer'

Above left 'Spode'

Left 'Snowfrost Pink'

'So Precious'

Above 'Stroke of Midnight'

Left 'Spring Willow Song'

Below 'Stop Sign'

'Siloam Double Classic' (Henry) Dor 40 cm (16 in) Dip E–M Re Fragrant bright pink double of outstanding quality in every way. Low, compact growth and prolific bloom make this gorgeous in a clump. This is very close to perfection for flower form and garden performance. It is one of the great all-time daylilies. *Photo p.17*

'Silver Ice' (Munson) S–Ev 63 cm (25 in) Tet E–M Re Pale icy pink flowers flushed lilac are produced on excellent plants. The growth is very vigorous and the flowers are large and ruffled. This is one of the best cultivars in the pale pink colours. It has proven to be very popular.

'Silver Sprite' (Munson) Ev 50 cm (20 in) Tet M Re Broad, ruffled lilac-lavender with a chalky lilac eye. Large flowers on good plants. This daylily produces a large number of proliferations in the Dural garden and is a nice addition to what is now an overcluttered class with many 'lookalikes'. It is fertile.

'Silverado' (Benz) S–Ev 50 cm (20 in) Tet M Unusually formed near white with heavy texture, ruffling and rounded petals. While the bloom is pretty the flowering period is short and the bloom sparse.

'Simply Pretty' (Sellers) S–Ev 80 cm (32 in) Tet M Re The outstanding apricot daylily for form growth and bloom production. The large ruffled flowers are a deep persimmon-apricot and are produced on excellent scapes. It is a landscaping dream and, as such, is highly recommended for quality and quantity. For us it is fully evergreen.

'Sir Prize' (Brown) Ev 68 cm (27 in) Tet E Re Large, flat, ruffled apricot-gold flowers of excellent quality are produced on strong scapes which often exceed their registered height in the Dural garden. This daylily makes a real statement in the garden.

'Sky Kissed' (Gates) Ev 45 cm (18 in) Dip E–M Re Beautiful bright lavender-purple bitone with a silver cast often exceeds its registered height at Dural. The rounded and ruffled flowers are particularly attractive. Excellent growth and production ensure this is highly recommended.

'Snow Bride' (Gates) Ev 50 cm (20 in) Dip E Re Very ruffled near white with an ivory-pink blush. The substance is excellent and repeat bloom is very good. *Photo p.44*

'Snowed In' (Millikan) Ev 63 cm (25 in) Dip M Flat, rounded and overlapping petals form a circle of white. The quality is excellent, as is the growth.

'Snowfrost Pink' (Pierce) S–Ev 55 cm (22 in) Dip M Re Bright clear pink of excellent quality. The flat, rounded and ruffled blooms are large and produced in profusion. This is a quality landscape or specimen pink daylily and more generous in its repeat bloom than 'Blue Happiness'. It is highly recommended for those many daylily enthusiasts who love pink flowers. *Photo p.116*

'So Fine' (Stamile) Ev 76 cm (30 in) Dip E–M Re Ruffled, clear rose-pink with a large green throat that spills out onto the petals. This is a quality daylily in every way and is well named.

'So Precious' (Stamile) S–Ev 70 cm (28 in) Tet E–M Re This rose-pink is outstanding and is a great personal favourite. Beautiful large ruffled flowers are produced on quality scapes. One of the very best in the clear pink class and a daylily that continually draws you back to it. I love the beautiful sheen to the petals. *Photo p.117*

'Solano Bull's Eye' (McFarland) Ev 50 cm (20 in) Dip E–M Re Large ruffled yellow with a red eye zone is spectacular in the garden and will grow to twice its registered height in the Dural garden where it is a beacon for all those lovers of eyed daylilies. *Photo p.33*

'Something Wonderful' (Salter) Ev 70 cm (28 in) Tet M Re Large, heavily ruffled ivory-cream with a yellow-green throat and gold edge. Beautiful, large, ruffled flowers ensure that it is particularly well named. This daylily was beautiful as seen in the hybridiser's Florida garden and it seems to have settled in to Australian conditions. It has excellent substance and super scapes. Fertile and an excellent parent.

'Sorcerer' (Talbott) Ev 76 cm (30 in) Dip M–L Re This is an excellent daylily with flowers of great size and excellent carrying power coupled with scapes which regularly exceed their registered height. It is superb in the latter part of the season and the colour is a tangerine-sherbet-pink with a deep rose-pink eye zone. *Photo p.116*

'Southern Love' (Sikes) Dor 76 cm (30 in) Dip M Rounded flesh-pink which is nicely ruffled. This daylily has proven to be a satisfactory, if not spectacular, grower.

'Southern Sunset' (Sellers) Dor 70 cm (28 in) Dip M–L Shrimp-rose with a strong yellow band of ruffling. The large flowers are produced on excellent plants which grow with ease.

'Splendid Touch' (Stamile) Ev 65 cm (26 in) Tet E–M Re Pale pink with a deeper pink halo with large ruffled flowers that are fragrant. Beautiful round form, lovely colour and good garden habits ensure popularity for this daylily. Substance is heavy and repeat bloom is excellent. It has proven to be very fertile.

'Spode' (Munson) Ev 80 cm (32 in) Tet M–L Re Large stunning pale lavender-pink with a green throat of extraordinary beauty. The rounded ruffled flowers are carried on tall scapes and are beautiful throughout the season. This is one of the best daylilies in the pastel shades and is ideal for specimen or mass planting. It is a personal favourite for its colour, form and all-round performance. *Photo p. 116*

'Spring Willow Song' (Munson) Ev 65 cm (26 in) Tet E–M Re Lemon-yellow with a small green throat. Large, ruffled blooms come on excellent scapes and the plant develops excellent clumps. Super quality plants and lovely bloom result in this being a top quality daylily. *Photo p. 116*

'Stop Sign' (Millikan) Dor 73 cm (29 in) Tet M–L Well named! The large ruffled dark red blooms bring garden visitors to a stop. Top quality flowers are spectacular in a clump. *Photo p. 117*

'Stroke of Midnight' (Kirchoff) Ev 63 cm (25 in) Dip E Re Deep wine-red double of excellent quality. The large flowers have a velvety texture and are consistently double once established. This is one of the best daylilies for specimen or landscape planting where a tall, dark red is required. It is highly recommended as an outstanding contrast for lighter colours. *Photo p. 117*

'Stronghold' (Brown) Ev 80 cm (32 in) Tet E–M Re Unusual contrasting fancy bicolour in orange-red and light orange. Large flowers are ruffled and spectacular in the garden on tall well-branched scapes.

'Strutter's Ball' (Moldovan) Dor 70 cm (28 in) Tet M Re Dark purple with a small silver watermark and lemon throat. This is a lovely daylily of excellent quality and is ideal for cold climates. It has been the best dark purple dormant cultivar.

'Study in Scarlet' (Kirchoff) Ev 70 cm (28 in) Tet E Re The clear blood-red blooms with green throats are a standout for colour and are wide and ruffled. Scapes are well branched and growth is good. The scapes are taller than those of 'Scarlet Orbit' and the plant is less floriferous. They are beautiful when grown together. *Photo p. 21*

'Sun Lord' (Blyth) Dor 80 cm (32 in) Tet E–M Wide and ruffled brilliant gold. The large flowers present a garden spectacle with very rich colouration and good garden habits.

'Sunset Loa' (Soules) S–Ev to Dor 60 cm (24 in) Tet M Bright apricot-pink with a darker apricot watermarked eye zone. This daylily is quite attractive in a clump.

'Sunset Strut' (Kirchoff) S–Ev 70 cm (28 in) Tet E–M Re Bright yellow-orange with a rose-violet eye zone. Large blooms are lightly ruffled and are of good quality on excellent scapes. Growth is good. *Photo p. 41*

'Surprisingly Pink' (Pierce) Dor 45 cm (18 in) Dip E–M Ruffled pale pink blend with darker ribbing and edging. Unusual colour pattern and very attractive individual blooms. Although this daylily has proven popular it is somewhat shy of bloom and not quick to increase.

'Sweet Shalimar' (Hansen) Ev 60 cm (24 in) Dip M Re Large, ruffled deep persimmon with orange veining. This is a top quality flower on a very good productive plant. The distinctive veining ensures the flower's individuality.

'Tani' (Pierce) S–Ev Dip 60 cm (24 in) E–M Unusual rose-pink with darker veining and a green throat. The large blooms are of excellent form but the plant is not particularly robust and bloom is sparse.

'Test Print' (Sellers) S–Ev 70 cm (28 in) Tet M Very large, full-formed lemon flowers are stunning in a clump. This is a quality daylily which produces a mass of bloom. *Photo p. 41*

'Timeless Fire' (Guidry) Ev 45 cm (18 in) Dip M Re Fragrant blood-red with a yellow throat. Large diamond-dusted flowers. *Photo p. 116*

'Totally Awesome' (Ward) Ev 70 cm (28 in) Dip E–M Re Rose-pink blend with a green throat. The huge double flowers are fragrant. I have not grown this cultivar.

'Touched by Midas'

'Tropic Sunset'

'Zimbabwe Sunset'

'Wildest Dreams'

'Zulu'

'Vino di Notte'

'Violet Osbome'

'Watermelon Moon'

'Walking on Sunshine'

'Venetian Splendor'

'Touched by Midas' (Winniford) Ev 76 cm (30 in) Tet E–M Re Magnificent rich gold of lovely form and excellent garden habits. Large flowers on good scapes and strong plants with beautiful foliage make this a landscaping special. For all-round performance I rate this the best gold and one of the very best of all daylilies. It is highly recommended and should be one of the first daylilies in any collection. *Photo p. 120*

'Trappist Monk' (Moldovan) S–Ev 55 cm (22 in) Tet E Re Vibrant smooth rose-coral and deep orange-salmon blend of excellent quality. This daylily grows well and flowers well. It is very attractive in a clump.

'Trogon' (Peck) S–Ev 63 cm (25 in) Tet M Large flame-red with wavy fringed ruffles and a darker blotch eye zone. This daylily forms an attractive clump.

'Trond' (Peck) Dor 68 cm (27 in) Tet M Rounded and velvety textured bright red of intense and distinctive colour. 'Trond' is very suitable for colder climates.

'Tropic Sunset' (Harris-Benz) Dor 60 cm (24 in) Tet E–M Very large and heavily ruffled rich coral-rose with a faint watermark. This is one of the loveliest daylilies in its colour range. 'Tropic Sunset' is ideal for cool to cold climates and has excellent substance. *Photo p. 120*

'Tropical Centrepiece' (Kirchoff) S–Ev 55 cm (22 in) Dip E Re Medium-sized rose-pink double with a red eye zone, this daylily was beautiful as seen in Florida and is now well settled in Australia. *Photo p. 10*

'Trudy Harris' (Harris-Benz) S–Ev 70 cm (28 in) Tet M Large ruffled rose-pink of lovely rounded form. This is an attractive flower in a delightful shade of pink. Plant habits are satisfactory and it is fertile.

'Tuscawilla Princess' (Hansen) S–Ev to Dor 65 cm (26 in) Dip M–L Re Peach-pink with a tiny olive-green heart. Large ruffled flowers on good scapes with plentiful bloom but growth is only average. *Photo p. 45*

'Twin Classic' (Kirchoff) Ev 76 cm (30 in) Dip M Re Large light but bright yellow double with a green throat. Bloom is prolific on the tall, well-budded scapes but the flowers are loosely held. This daylily is excellent in a massed display.

'Undulata' (Millikan) S–Ev 55 cm (22 in) Dip M Re Large, full and ruffled cream of quality. Excellent growth and productivity are major factors in its acceptance as a good garden plant.

'Vanilla Candy' (Stamile) Dor 58 cm (23 in) Tet M Ruffled and rounded cream with a red eye. This is one of a series of 'Candy' daylilies each with contrasting eyes. Growth and plant habits are satisfactory.

'Vanity Case' (Millikan) Ev 45 cm (18 in) Dip M–L Ruffled green-yellow of quality. This daylily is very pretty in a clump. It is, however, in a class that is overcrowded.

'Venetian Magistrate' (Munson) Ev 60 cm (24 in) Tet E–M Re Lavender-mauve with a chartreuse throat. This is an attractive flower, large and nicely patterned on a plant that grows with ease and performs well.

'Venetian Splendor' (Munson) S–Ev 60 cm (24 in) Tet M Re Bicolour in rosy mauve and yellow-gold with a bold plum-purple eye. Flowers are large and lightly ruffled. Plant habits are good. *Photo p. 121*

'Vi Simmons' (Talbott) Ev 60 cm (24 in) Dip M Re Lovely large flowered baby-ribbon pink of excellent quality. The fragrant blooms are of beautiful clear colour and the plant performs well. *Photo p. 44*

'Victoria's Secret' (Salter) S–Ev 70 cm (28 in) Tet M–L Re This is one of the most attractive edged varieties. Colour is a pastel pink with a gold edge. Blooms are large, ruffled and are often double in warmer weather. It is a personal favourite as one often observes single and double blooms in the same clump. Scapes are well-branched. Fertile. *Photo p. 45*

'Vino di Notte' (Kirchoff) Ev 80 cm (32 in) Tet E Re Rich dark purple with a lime-green throat. Large blooms on excellent scapes, which can grow tall, make a wonderful display on a very healthy, vigorous plant. This is my favourite dark purple and is highly recommended for a specimen planting or for a large display of tall dark purple flowers. It is fertile. *Photo p. 121*

'Vintage Bordeaux' (Kirchoff) Ev 68 cm (27 in) Tet E Re Rich black-cherry with a chartreuse throat on large flowers produced in profusion. The form is wide and ruffled and the vigorous plants multiply quickly. This is one of the best dark varieties for mass landscaping display.

'Violet Osborne' (Kirchoff) Ev 58 cm (23 in) Dip E Re Peach-pink double with a red eye zone and green heart. Large, well-formed, fragrant flowers are consistently double and bloom is prolific. This is an eyecatching variety. *Photo p. 121*

'Virginia Peck' (Durio) Ev 70 cm (28 in) Tet E Re Large near white with a rose-red edge and green throat. This is unusual, attractive and vigorous. *Photo p.37*

'Walking on Sunshine' (Salter) Ev 55 cm (22 in) Tet E–M Re Bright lemon-yellow with a tiny green heart. The flowers are large, rounded and ruffled. Quality is excellent and this will be popular when it is established. It is fertile and an excellent parent. *Photo p.121*

'Warmest Regards' (Harris-Benz) Ev 60 cm (24 in) Tet M Wide-formed and well-ruffled deep rose-pink. Large flowers and satisfactory garden performance ensure popularity.

'Watermelon Moon' (Stamile) Dor 68 cm (27 in) Tet M–L Large melon-pink blend with an orange throat. This is a quality daylily that is a most attractive colour. *Photo p.121*

'Wedding Band' (Stamile) Ev 65 cm (26 in) Tet M Re Quality, fragrant creamy white-edged yellow with a green throat. Outstanding in every way—one of the best! I admired this daylily in the hybridiser's garden in Florida and am delighted with its performance since importing it. Fertile and an excellent parent. *Photo p.37*

'Westminster Lace' (Salter) S–Ev 70 cm (28 in) Tet M Re Very beautiful pale pink with a wide gold picotee edge. The large blooms are full, overlapped, ruffled and crepe-textured. Excellent scapes carry many buds. This daylily grows well and performs well. It is one of the loveliest picotee pastels and is highly recommended for garden display or specimen planting. *Photo p.45*

'White Crinoline' (Stamile) Dor 52 cm (21 in) Tet E–M Re Fragrant white 15 cm (6 in) blooms with a green heart. This is a very attractive near white for garden display. *Photo p.33*

'White Tie Affair' (Peck) Dor 60 cm (24 in) Tet M Re Nicely formed white of quality. Large rounded flowers on good quality plants but flower production is only moderate.

'Whooperee' (Gates) Ev 60 cm (24 in) Tet E Re Bright rose-red with a darker eye zone and chalky green throat. The ruffled and recurved blooms are of exceptional quality and this daylily presents a garden spectacle. It is a distinctly different red and a very worthy daylily for specimen or massed planting. *Photo p.44*

'Wildest Dreams' (Temple) Ev 65 cm (26 in) Dip E Re Simple huge classic spider bloom is rose-pink and yellow on the outer parts of the flower with a very large green throat. Flower parts are long and slender. If you like them big and spidery, this is for you! It grows and flowers well. *Photo p.120*

'William Austin Morris' (Salter) S–Ev 70 cm (28 in) Tet E–M Re Mid pink blend with a green throat. Large, full, round flowers are ruffled. This is a pretty daylily worth a place in any collection. It is vigorous, produces good scapes and is very fertile.

'Wind Frills' (Tarrant) Ev 108 cm (43 in) Dip E–M–L Re This large pink daylily is a personal favourite of all the spider types available. It grows tall but is always attractive in the garden or landscape. Excellent quality for those who like the spidery type flowers, particularly as the flowers are held so well and the plant is vigorous. *Photo p.44*

'Wings of Tide' (Hansen) S–Ev 60 cm (24 in) Dip M–L Re Peach-pink with darker rose-pink veins and a dark lavender-blue eye zone and lacy gold edging. The medium-sized flowers are nicely formed and ruffled while the colour is most unusual. This is a worthy daylily. *Photo p.44*

'Woodside Ruby' (Apps) S–Ev 85 cm (34 in) Dip M Richly coloured ruby-red of nice form that is very attractive. The blooms are 11 cm (4.5 in) and as such, are on the borderline between small-flowered and large-flowered. *Photo p.10*

'Yazoo Soufflé' (Smith) Ev 65 cm (26 in) Dip E–M Re Shell-pink and ivory blended double with large, quality flowers that are consistently double. Excellent quality for those who like double flowers. *Photo p.40*

'Zimbabwe Sunset' (Hansen) S–Ev 60 cm (24 in) Dor M–L Re Large, ruffled hot pink and coral blend with a green throat. This is a very beautiful flower and the plant grows well. *Photo p.120*

'Zulu' (Grosvenor) Ev 70 cm (28 in) Tet M–L Re This is my one contribution to the recommended cultivars and it is a worthy representative. The dark wine-red to black-red flowers have a small, green throat surrounded by yellow to light up the bloom. These flowers are large, rounded, well-formed and ruffled. The well-branched scapes carry many blooms through a long flowering season. This quality dark daylily will be proudly grown for many years. It combines the best qualities of its parents, the illustrious 'Scarlet Orbit' and 'Vintage Bordeaux', and is an excellent specimen plant as well as being spectacular in a massed display. *Photo p.120*

Small-flowered and miniature daylilies

'Balaringar Helen' (Lee) Dor 45 cm (18 in) Dip E–M Re This is Margaret Lee's best small-flowered cultivar. The nicely rounded flowers are clear pink with a darker halo and a green throat. They have a velvety texture and are diamond-dusted. *Photo p. 128*

'Blue Moon Rising' (E Salter) S–Ev 60 cm (24 in) Dip M Re Small-flowered ivory-peach with a blue-violet eye zone and yellow-green throat. For colour alone this is a special daylily. *Photo p. 128*

'Blushing Maiden' (Kirchoff) Ev 65 cm (26 in) Dip E–M Re Beautiful pink bitone with ivory-pink sepals, pink petals and a yellow-green throat. Lovely in a garden clump.

'Bumble Bee' (Williamson) Ev 30 cm (12 in) Dip VE Re Tiny yellow with a rose eye. This is an older but still nice daylily. *Photo p. 132*

'Butterfly Ballet' (Dunbar) Ev 70 cm (28 in) Dip E–M Re Outstanding ruffled and crimped golden-yellow flowers are at the upper end for small flower classification. Quality is excellent for landscaping where it produces a mass of colour.

'Butterfly Charm' (Dunbar) Ev 45 cm (18 in) Dip E–M Re Vibrant, clear butter-yellow with waxy substance and full round form. This daylily is lower growing than 'Butterfly Ballet' and equally beautiful in the landscape. *Photo p. 170*

'Butterscotch Ruffles' (Harling) S–Ev 60 cm (24 in) Dip E Re Butterscotch blended small flower that is rounded and ruffled and blooms over a long period. This prolific daylily produces a great display of subdued colour.

'Come See' (Hansen) S–Ev 45 cm (18 in) Dip M Re Small-flowered blue-lavender with a blue-lilac halo. Unusual and attractive colour sets this daylily apart. It is attractive in its own right but is also very useful as a foil for the rich colours. *Photo p. 132*

Opposite 'Crimson Icon'

'Coming Up Roses' (Hager) Ev 76 cm (30 in) Dip E Re This is the best rose-pink small-flowered daylily. The wide, rounded flowers are richly coloured, lightly ruffled and produced in profusion on well-branched scapes with up to 25 buds. It is superb in every way but is particularly useful as a landscape display for massed colour. *Photo p. 132*

'Crimson Icon' (Hudson) S–Ev 38 cm (15 in) Dip M Re This very bright red with a yellow-green throat is a long-time favourite. It is a landscaping special where a red mini is required as the colour is so attractive. *Photo opposite*

'Cupid's Gold' (Hudson) S–Ev 33 cm (13 in) Dip M Re This gorgeous little yellow-gold mini produces tiny flowers in profusion to provide a mound of colour. Excellent landscaper for a low-growing mass of yellow over an extended period. It has been used extensively for landscaping.

'Dark Avenger' (E Salter) S–Ev 45 cm (18 in) Dip M Re Superb dark red on exceptional branched scapes with plenty of bloom. Garden habits are good and this is one of the best small flowers for all-round performance. *Photo p. 132*

'Daughter of Destiny' (E Salter) S–Ev 60 cm (24 in) Tet E–M Orange with a red eye zone and green throat. This is one of the new tetraploid small flowers and is an excellent garden performer as a specimen or for landscaping.

'Dorothy Stacks' (Lewis) Dor 60 cm (24 in) Tet M Small-flowered, rounded and lightly ruffled dark red self. The flower is larger than 'Dark Avenger' and the garden effect less satisfying.

'Dragon's Dreams' (E Salter) S–Ev 63 cm (25 in) Dip M–L Re Rounded lavender with a washed blue-lavender eye. The small flowers are, at times, double and are well-formed. This is a pretty daylily. *Photo p. 148*

'Dragon's Eye' (E Salter) S–Ev 55 cm (22 in) Dip M L Re This beautiful daylily borders on the small-flowered class. Blooms are 9–10 cm (3½–4 in) pale rose-pink with a rose-red eye and lime-green throat. Prolific and very attractive. It is the rich colour of this flower that is so very appealing. *Photo p.130*

'Dragon's Orb' (E Salter) S–Ev 50 cm (20 in) Dip M Re Lovely ivory mini with a black eye zone and green throat. Great colour contrast makes this a special daylily for colour.

'Elfin Escapade' (Hudson) Ev 40 cm (16 in) Dip M–L Pale ivory tiny blooms with a sharply defined plum-black eye. This stunning daylily is very eye catching both as a specimen or in massed display. It grows well. *Photo p.152*

'Elfin Etching' (E Salter) S–Ev 50 cm (20 in) Dip M–L Pale ivory-cream with a large washed lavender eye that is etched and veined purple. Lovely, rounded small flower of beautiful colour combination on a plant that performs well. *Photo p.129*

'Elfin Imp' (Hudson) Ev 33 cm (13 in) Dip E–M Re This is one of the finest miniatures. The lovely crepe-textured blooms are golden-yellow and provide a mass of colour. All plant habits are excellent and this is a landscape special. *Photo p.130*

'Enchanter's Spell' (Hudson) Ev 45 cm (18 in) Dip M Re Magnificent small flowers of pale ivory-white with a multi-layered eye pattern. I have loved this colour pattern since first seeing it and my enthusiasm is shared by others.

'Exotic Echo' (Sellers) Dor 40 cm (16 in) Dip M Re Super quality flower with a triple eye zone in shades of burgundy on a cream base. Growth and plant habits are good but it is the colour pattern that really attracts. *Photo p.130*

'Fairy Filigree' (E Salter) S–Ev 80 cm (32 in) Tet M–L Re Creamy yellow small flower with a lime heart and heavily ruffled gold edge. The flower form and colour are special but the flowering spikes and size of bloom lack balance. It is nevertheless a garden special for colour and form. *Photo p.157*

'Fairy Firecracker' (Hudson) Ev 38 cm (15 in) Dip M Beautiful bicolour in red and yellow with intense colouring. This is one of the most attractive miniatures and it grows well. I love the colour combination and find this one of the nicest miniatures for massed display.

'Fairy Frosting' (Hudson) Ev 38 cm (15 in) Dip E–M Re Tiny ivory and pale frosty pink blend. Plentiful bloom and good plant habits make this a very valuable pastel.

'Flower Fiesta' (Kirchoff) Dor 45 cm (18 in) Dip E Re This small daylily has an unusual colouring of vermilion with a red eye zone. Growth and vigour are good.

'Guinivere's Gift' (E Salter) Ev 45 cm (18 in) Tet M Re Cool lemon-yellow with a green throat and ruffled gold edges. Scapes are well-branched and the garden effect is beautiful. This is one of the new range of small-flowered tetraploids that are destined to become very popular. *Photo p.129*

'Heart of Jade' (Kennedy) Dor 55 cm (22 in) Dip M Small-flowered deep pink with rose-pink veins and a jade-green throat. The velvet-textured blooms are unique for colour and form. Although the flower form is neither wide nor rounded this daylily is a very welcome addition to the pink range. *Photo p.131*

'Heart's Glee' (Kirchoff) S–Ev 60 cm (24 in) Dip E–M Re Small flowers are white and most attractive. The blooms are rounded, ruffled and crimped. Growth is good as are all the plant habits. This daylily has proven most popular. *Photo p.160*

'Ivory Venus' (Steinborn) Ev 60 cm (24 in) Dip M Pale ivory-cream with round, ruffled form. This is a pretty daylily in a very popular colour. It grows and flowers well. *Photo p.130*

'Jason Salter' (E Salter) Ev 45 cm (18 in) Dip E–M Re This is one of the very best minis in pale creamy yellow with an etched eye pattern of washed raisin-plum and a darker pencil edge. Everything about this daylily is quality (the flowers, the scape, the growth, the increase). It is sensational when viewed as a large clump or in a massed display. *Photo p.129*

'Jewelled Sunbeam' (E Salter) Ev 38 cm (15 in) Dip E–M Re Tiny, delicate, rounded and ruffled pure yellow of outstanding quality. Grows well and flowers well. Beautiful in a clump. I recommend this miniature for clear colour, good form and excellent performance. *Photo p.131*

'Jim McGinnis' (Hudson) Ev 38 cm (15 in) Dip E–M Pale peach-pink with a bold intense rose-red eye zone. This is a most colourful flower and is prolific when in bloom although the bloom season is shorter than most of the miniatures.

'Knick Knack' (Hudson) S–Ev to Dor 35 cm (14 in) Dip E–M Tiny flowers are orange-gold with a green throat. Prolific bloom makes a great garden display. This is lovely in a clump where it is a mass of bloom. It is one of the very best miniatures. *Photo p. 134*

'Lady Limelight' (Hudson) Ev 35 cm (14 in) Dip L Small-flowered ivory which puts on a great display late in the season. Quality growth and vigour but only a limited bloom season.

'Lady Moonlight' (E Salter) S–Ev 50 cm (20 in) Tet M Re Very lovely pale creamy white of exceptional quality. The blooms are full, wide, rounded and overlapping while the scapes are multi-budded. This is a special small-flowered variety for flower form and is one of the best of the new tetraploid miniatures. *Photo p. 133*

'Ladykin' (Kennedy) Dor 55 cm (22 in) Dip M–L Bicolour of soft pink and white. The ruffled small flowers are most attractive and this daylily is a sell-out wherever we can build up sufficient stock to list it in our catalogue. It is very popular and deservedly so because of its most attractive pink colour.

'Leprechaun's Lace' (Hudson) Dor 38 cm (15 in) Dip M Re Creped and ruffled creamy peach-pink of outstanding quality. The tiny flowers are crepe textured and produced in profusion on excellent scapes. This daylily is superb in every way and is one of the best for landscaping or massed display because of the quantity and quality of bloom. It has proven very popular. *Photo p. 133*

'Lilliputian Knight' (Hudson) Ev 40 cm (16 in) Dip M–L Re Tiny rose-red flowers are produced in profusion on excellent scapes. This is a quality landscaping daylily that grows and increases very well and puts on a wonderful display.

'Lilting Lady' (Stevens) Dor 50 cm (20 in) Tet M–L Small-flowered pale rose-pink with a rose-red eye zone on excellent scapes. Bloom is prolific although a little large for the class. It is one of those in-between daylilies for flower size but well worth growing.

'Little Christine' (Croker) Dor 45 cm (18 in) Dip E–M Re This is a dark red beauty with a black-red eye zone. Flowers border on the small flower size and are produced in profusion. Excellent for anyone who wants a quality dark red miniature as a specimen or for massed display.

'Little Fairy Festival' (E Salter) S–Ev 45 cm (18 in) Dip M Re Attractive mini of unusual colouring. Flowers are cream overlaid with orange-red stippling and are very appealing—much like the plicata pattern in bearded iris. *Photo p. 134*

'Little Fat Cat' (Brown) S–Ev 65 cm (26 in) E–M Quality, rounded and ruffled near white, small-flowered cultivar. The wide petals and lovely form make this a special daylily. The flowers have an appealing texture and the colour is most distinctive.

'Little Fat Dazzler' (Lankart) S–Ev 40 cm (16 in) Dip E–M Rounded and ruffled small flower in light rosy red with a green throat. Prolific bloom makes this a special daylily. This is an older daylily that is still worth a place in the garden. *Photo p. 134*

'Little Grapette' (Williamson) S–Ev 30 cm (12 in) Dip E Re Tiny, rounded grape-purple with a green throat. Well-balanced plant with tiny flowers and neat, grassy foliage. This is an older daylily that is still worth a place in the garden.

'Little Greenie' (Winniford) Dor 45 cm (18 in) Dip M Well-formed, rounded green-yellow small flower. Spikes are well-branched and growth is good. The overall effect is quite green-toned.

'Little Gypsy Vagabond' (Cruse) Ev 45 cm (18 in) Dip E–M Creamy yellow small flower with a near black eye zone and a green throat. Prolific bloom and excellent growth make this a winner both for individual planting and mass landscaping.

'Little Joy' (Lewis) Dor 70 cm (28 in) Dip M Blood-red small flower on tall spikes. The flowers are set off with a darker eye zone. Although I prefer 'Little Christine' in this colour range, 'Little Joy' is well worth growing.

'Little Zinger' (Lankart) S–Ev to Dor 40 cm (16 in) Dip E–M Rounded clear red blooms in profusion. This is a good landscaping daylily that will be dormant in colder areas.

'Lullaby Baby' (Spalding) Dor 48 cm (19 in) Dip E–M Long-time favourite small flower in pale pink. The ruffled flowers are perfectly formed and most attractive. Although this is an older daylily its quality has ensured continued popularity. *Photo opposite*

'Magic Masquerade' (Salter) S–Ev 40 cm (16 in) Dip M Re Very ruffled pale creamy yellow with a deep raisin-plum eye zone produced on excellent show scapes. This is a beautiful daylily and an excellent grower which produces a mass of bloom. It is very highly recommended.

'Blue Moon Rising'

'Maleny Debutante' *Photograph by Scott Alexander*

'Balaringar Helen'

'Bumble Bee'

'Guinivere's Gift'

'Jason Salter'

'Elfin Etching'

'Exotic Echo'

'Dragon's Eye'

Right 'Elfin Imp'

'Ivory Venus'

'Heart of Jade'

'Jewelled Sunbeam'

'Siloam Robbie Bush'

Right 'Dark Avenger'

'Tropical Tangerine'

'Come See'

'Coming Up Roses'

'Leprechaun's Lace'

'Lullaby Baby'

'Lady Moonlight'

'Little Fat Dazzler'

'Knick Knack'

'Little Fairy Festival'

Opposite 'Moonlight Mist'

'Magician's Mask' (E Salter) Ev 55 cm (22 in) Dip M Re Small flower in pale yellow-gold with a bold black eye and lime throat. Form is full, round and ruffled. The colour pattern is spectacular. *Photo p. 138*

'Maleny Debutante' (Alexander) Ev 70 cm (28 in) Dip E Re Clear pastel peach with a bright rose-red eye zone and green throat. Full, round and ruffled form with well-branched, recurrent scapes and vigorous growth make this a special daylily. *Photo p. 128*

'Mambo Maid' (Faggard) Ev 48 cm (19 in) Dip E–M This is a favourite small-flowered orange daylily. The flowers are texture-veined with a darker orange eye and are stunning for colour. Scapes are good and so is the growth. I highly recommend this as one of the best landscaping and massed display daylilies. *Photo opposite*

'Matchmaking Miss' (E Salter) S–Ev 60 cm (24 in) Dip M Re Small-flowered bright rose-pink with a bold eye of rose-red around a lime-green throat. Form is round, full and overlapped but it is the striking colour which makes this a standout. *Photo p. 138*

'Meadow Sprite' (Hudson) Ev 33 cm (13 in) Dip M Re Pretty small flower in lilac to rosy lavender with a deeper eye. This is a most attractive daylily which retains its popularity even among more recent introductions. *Photo p. 138*

'Moonlight Mist' (Hudson) Ev 40 cm (16 in) Dip M–L Re This is one of the great daylilies! The full, rounded, ruffled and overlapping blooms are a soft blend of ivory and creamy pink giving a light pink effect. Bloom, scapes, growth, vigour and production are all great. Superb! *Photo p. 133*

'Morrie Otte' (E Salter) S–Ev 45 cm (18 in) Dip M Re Very attractive lavender-mauve-purple with a precise silvery frosted lavender eye. This unique daylily is a colour gem. *Photo opposite*

'Mosel' (Kirchoff) Ev 45 cm (18 in) Dip E Re This is the 'whitest' of the white mini to small flowers. Form is round, ruffled and overlapping. Growth, vigour, increase and re-bloom are all excellent and 'Mosel' has proven one of the best landscaping daylilies. Recommended.

'Mystic Moon' (E Salter) S–Ev 45 cm (18 in) Tet M–L Re Tiny pale ivory-cream tetraploid brings a new dimension to this class. Form is full and round and the ruffled flowers are crepe textured. Well-branched scapes, vigorous plants and a delightful colour will ensure popularity. *Photo opposite*

'Ono' (Johnson) Ev 45 cm (18 in) Dip E–M Very ruffled light yellow small to medium-sized flower. It is most attractive as a clump and is very suitable for landscaping.

'Paris Lace' (Salter) Ev 45 cm (18 in) Dip E–M Re Tiny, round and very ruffled pale cream dusted yellow. Flowers are produced on excellent scapes with numerous buds. This is a true miniature that is superb as a rockery plant.

'Pastel Accent' (Sellers) Dor 60 cm (24 in) Dip M Re Small-flowered pale pink with a subtle darker pink eye. The soft-coloured flowers are exquisite, the plants grow well and this is very popular.

'Pat Croker' (Croker) Dor 65 cm (26 in) Dip E–M Small-flowered pink of exquisite colour. The blooms are round, ruffled and beautiful. Supply never meets demand for this most attractive pink daylily.

'Patchwork Puzzle' (Salter) Ev 45 cm (18 in) Dip E–M Rounded pale ivory-lemon with a fine pencil etched purple eye surrounding a lighter washed eye of pale ivory-lavender and lemon. This superb daylily has excellent garden habits and is outstanding in the garden for specimen planting or massed display. It is very highly recommended. *Photo p. 166*

'Picadilly Princess' (E Salter) Ev 45 cm (18 in) Tet M Re Delicate peach-pink with a rose-red eye and green throat. The full-formed, rounded and ruffled small flowers are produced in profusion over a long period and this is an outstanding performer. *Photos p. 141, 156*

'Powder and Paint' (Millikan) Ev 50 cm (20 in) Dip E Nicely rounded light cream with a bright rose-red eye and green throat.

'Prince Redbird' (Sellers) Dor 65 cm (26 in) Tet M Re This is the best red small-flowered daylily! Brilliant red colouration coupled with round, ruffled blooms on excellent scapes make this near perfection. Outstanding garden performance in every way makes this a real winner. It is very highly recommended. *Photo p. 142*

'Pudgie' (Winniford) Dor 40 cm (16 in) Dip M Attractive small-flowered green-yellow double that is very well suited to colder climates.

'Purple Pinwheel' (Kennedy) Dor 55 cm (22 in) Dip E–M This is a most unusual and beautiful daylily! It is a purple bitone with white midribs and makes a starting contrast in the garden to other colours because of the unique pattern. *Photo p. 141*

'Mystic Moon'

'Mambo Maid'

Right 'Morrie Otte'

'Magician's Mask'

'Matchmaking Miss'

'Meadow Sprite'

'Saucy Rogue'

'Siloam David Kirchoff'

'Siloam Bertie Ferris'

'Renegade Lady' (E Salter) Ev 70 cm (28 in) Dip M–L Re Bright golden-yellow flower with a large red eye and tiny green throat. The ruffled flowers are full and rounded. The colour is sensational and this will be very popular once it is established in Australia. *Photo p. 142*

'Robbie Salter' (Kirchoff) Ev 60 cm (24 in) Dip M Re Mid coral-pink with a darker coral band and pie-crust ruffles edged in buff-pink.

'Royal Fanfare' (Kirchoff) Ev 50 cm (20 in) Dip E Re Smallish flower of raspberry with a wide coral buff-pink halo. This is another of those in-between flowers, too big for a small flower, too small for a large flower.

'Saucy Rogue' (Hudson) S–Ev 40 cm (16 in) Dip M Re Tiny flowers in deep rose-red are produced in profusion on excellent scapes. Grows well and because of its productivity it is a good landscape plant. *Photo p. 139*

'Scruples' (Kirchoff) Ev 55 cm (22 in) Dip E Re Full, recurved small flowers in amber tones with a pink overlay. Grows well.

'Siloam Baby Talk' (Henry) Dor 38 cm (15 in) Dip E–M Full-formed small flower in pale pink with a deep rose-pink eye. Growth and vigour are excellent and this is a mass of colour but the bloom period is unfortunately short.

'Siloam Bertie Ferris' (Henry) S–Ev 40 cm (16 in) Dip E–M Lovely heavily ruffled blend of rose, red and copper with a darker eye. Makes a delightful mound of colour in the garden, as it grows quite low in my garden. The blooms are very well-formed and rounded and this is an excellent cultivar for a rockery. *Photo p. 139*

'Siloam Bo Peep' (Henry) Ev 45 cm (18 in) Dip E–M Re Small-flowered cream and pink blend with a deep purple eye. Growth and garden habits are excellent. Lovely in a clump, this daylily produces a great display. *Photo p. 142*

'Siloam David Kirchoff' (Henry) Dor 40 cm (16 in) Dip E–M Re Beautiful lavender with a shaded purple eye and a green throat. This is a most attractive small-flowered daylily and a personal favourite for colour and pattern. It is highly recommended because of its beautiful colour pattern and all-round performance. *Photo p. 139*

'Siloam Dream Baby' (Henry) S–Ev 45 cm (18 in) Dip M Re Full-formed and rounded small flowers in soft apricot with a deep purple eye zone on a scape with excellent branching. Growth is very vigorous and increase is quick. This is a lovely daylily and is highly recommended as one of the best small flowers. *Photo p. 160*

'Siloam Jim Cooper' (Henry) Dor 40 cm (16 in) Dip E–M Very special, rounded and ruffled red which darkens around the green throat. It is very low-growing for me and the blooms are of outstanding quality and colour.

'Siloam Merle Kent' (Henry) Dor 45 cm (18 in) Dip M Lovely small flower in bright orchid with a deep purple eye! This is a spectacular little daylily that is a pleasure to grow. It is very popular and deservedly so. *Photo p. 142*

'Siloam Red Ruby' (Henry) Dor 45 cm (18 in) Dip M Dark ruby-red self with a green throat. This small-flowered cultivar is at the upper limit for flower size but is very attractive in the garden where it provides excellent contrast for the lighter colours.

'Siloam Red Toy' (Henry) Dor 50 cm (20 in) Dip E–M Light red small flower with a green throat. This daylily grows well and is carried on well-branched scapes.

'Siloam Robbie Bush' (Henry) S–Ev 45 cm (18 in) Dip M Lovely small flower in rose-pink with a deep red eye zone. It is one of the nicest of the 'Siloams', being an excellent performer in every respect. The colour pattern is very attractive. *Photo p. 132*

'Siloam Valentine' (Henry) Dor 50 cm (20 in) Dip E–M Re Small-flowered red-apricot with a deeper eye and green throat. This pretty flower is easily grown as the garden habits are excellent.

'Siloam Virginia Henson' (Henry) Dor 45 cm (18 in) Dip E–M Small-flowered creamy pink with a ruby-red eye zone. While not spectacular in itself the converted tetraploid version of this daylily has proven an outstanding breeder for eyes and lovely rounded form.

'Sir Blackstem' (Hager) Ev 60 cm (24 in) Dip E Re The small flowers are orange-yellow with a brown reverse. The highlight is the unique stem on which these flowers are carried—it is deep black-purple and the buds are also dark. This daylily is a standout as a specimen and is also excellent for landscaping.

'Prince Redbird'

'Purple Pinwheel'

'Picadilly Princess'

'Renegade Lady'

'Siloam Bo Peep'

Left 'Tangerine Tango'

'Siloam Merle Kent'

'Tiny Temptress'

Left 'Toy Circus'

'Tiny Pumpkin'

Left 'Witch's Wink'

'Super Doll'

Left 'Tom Collins'

'Wee Wizard'

Left 'Tuscawilla Dave Talbott'

'Spell Fire' (E Salter) S–Ev 50 cm (20 in) Dip M Re Bright yellow small flower with an intense red eye zone. Form is round and recurved but it is the colour which is so special.

'Sugar Cookie' (Apps) Ev 53 cm (21 in) Dip E–M Luscious cream small flowers are carried on well-branched scapes. Growth and performance are excellent and this is a very popular daylily.

'Sugar Doll' (Joiner) Dor 60 cm (24 in) Dip E–M Re Yellow with a pale red eye zone. Small flowers are heavily substanced and nicely ruffled. Growth, health and vigour are all good.

'Summer Echoes' (Hansen) Ev 50 cm (20 in) Dip M–L Re Creamy apricot small flowers with a large wine-purple eye. This is a lovely, heavy-blooming daylily very suitable for massed display.

'Super Doll' (Joiner) S–Ev 50 cm (20 in) Dip E Re Superb small-flowered soft apricot with a green throat. The fragrant blooms are well-formed and ruffled. Garden performance is excellent in every way. This is recommended as one of the very best performers. *Photo opposite*

'Sweet Pea' (Winniford) S–Ev 25 cm (10 in) Dip E–M Tiny yellow flowers with a pea-green throat. Foliage is thin and grassy and this daylily is excellent in a rockery. It is highly recommended for any situation where a small flower on a small plant is required.

'Tangerine Tango' (E Salter) S–Ev 60 cm (24 in) Tet E–M Re Spectacular light orange with a green throat. The small flowers are rounded and ruffled. Very beautiful in a clump and productive of a good garden display. *Photo p. 142*

'Tiny Pumpkin' (Hudson) Ev 50 cm (20 in) Dip E–M Re Rich intense orange self with a green throat. The lovely tiny flowers are carried in masses on quality scapes. This is one of the great landscaping daylilies and comes with the highest recommendation. *Photo p. 143*

'Tiny Talisman' (Hudson) S–Ev 40 cm (16 in) Dip M Re Tiny, recurved and rounded pale buff-ivory with a subtle eye of light plum. This is an easy growing plant. *Photo p. 162*

'Tiny Temptress' (E Salter) Ev 38 cm (15 in) Dip M Re Deep rose-pink mini with a red eye zone blooms in profusion. Quality is good both for flower production and beauty in the garden. *Photo p. 143*

'Tiny Trumpeter' (Hudson) Dor 40 cm (16 in) Dip M Re Tiny, velvety dark rose-red blooms are produced in abundance on an easy growing plant. *Photo p. 156*

'Tom Collins' (Millikan) Dor 65 cm (26 in) Dip E–M This small-flowered daylily is at the upper limit for flower size but it is sensational. The rounded, recurved yellow flowers are highlighted by green centres to give a beautiful effect. It is lovely for massed display or individual planting and is particularly good in colder climates. *Photo opposite*

'Toy Circus' (Mederer) S–Ev 50 cm (20 in) Dip E–M Re Unique bicolour in rose-red and bright yellow. The small flowers are rounded and ruffled and the garden effect is stunning. I just love the colour pattern of this daylily and highly recommend it for those who like something different. *Photo p. 143*

'Tropical Tangerine' (E Salter) Ev 50 cm (20 in) Tet M Re Super quality rich orange with salmon highlights. The excellent small-flowered variety is rounded and ruffled and is a beacon in the garden among the smaller daylilies. *Photo p. 128*

'Tropical Toy' (Hudson) Ev 50 cm (20 in) Dip M Re Full, rounded, small flower in soft creamy peach with a ruffled and crinkled edge. Lovely flowers on excellent scapes and prolific bloom make this a special daylily.

'Tuscawilla Dave Talbott' (Hansen) Ev 65 cm (26 in) Dip M Re Ruffled almond with a dark raisin-purple eye zone, picotee purple edge and green throat. For its excellent performance and unusual colour this quality rounded small flower is a personal favourite. It is a daylily to be observed close up for its gorgeous combination of colours. *Photo opposite*

'Velvet Shadows' (Hudson) S–Ev 38 cm (15 in) Dip M–L Rich plum-violet with a chalky lavender eye and a green throat. This dark small flower provides good contrast for the lighter colours.

'Wee Wizard' (E Salter) S–Ev 50 cm (20 in) Dip M Pale lavender with a large washed grey-lavender eye surrounded by a deep purple pencil edge. This is a top quality, ruffled small flower of distinctive colour pattern. *Photo opposite*

'Witch's Wink' (E Salter) Ev 65 cm (26 in) Tet E–M Re Stunning bright golden-yellow with a bold black-purple eye. This is a quality, rounded and ruffled small flower with great contrast between the yellow flower and the dark eye. *Photo p. 143*

7 Sources of supply

Daylilies are universally good growers and increase quickly. In most areas prospective growers should have no trouble growing, and growing well, any cultivars of their choice. However, care should be taken by growers in areas with climatic extremes. I would advise gardeners in very hot, tropical climates to consider evergreen cultivars initially, while those who live in very cold climates would be best served by dormant cultivars initially. Once you have gained experience you can then experiment and broaden the range you grow.

Growers have basically two sources for obtaining daylilies.

Nurseries

Intending buyers will often be able to obtain unnamed or very old cultivars or unnamed seedlings from non-specialist nurseries, sometimes at bargain prices. This can be a very satisfactory way to fill a spot in the garden. However, price should be a guide to quality. You should be wary of very cheap daylilies.

New release daylilies are very expensive. In the USA they usually range in price from US$50 to over US$200 with most in the range of US$75 to US$150. If you live somewhere other than the USA, then you should also remember that when you purchase a recently released USA-bred daylily from your nursery, this nursery has not only had to buy the plant from a supplier in the USA at a high price, but has also incurred high importation costs for certification, packing, freight, quarantine and growing-on fees.

Fortunately, daylilies are tough and take the shock of being moved even from one country to another reasonably well. In addition, daylilies are relatively disease-free and so losses are minimal. Most acclimatise to a new country quickly and it is not long before they are growing and increasing quickly. This means that a nursery which has imported a new variety can sometimes have it on the general market in two years from being imported. Hence the latest releases in one country can be available commercially in another country in two to four years after their initial release by the hybridiser. To do this, however, the nursery must be prepared to pay the high initial price put on new releases.

The price of a particular variety of daylily goes through a typical pattern. It starts out high but over subsequent years the price drops considerably. There has been much criticism of the very high prices expected for new release daylilies and the delay in the fall in prices. Some of this criticism is no doubt justified. On the other hand, when one considers that a hybridiser may have had to grow several thousand seedlings to produce that one special variety for release, then the time, expertise and 'land use' to produce that special cultivar would justify the high initial asking price.

In my view, a more important and major problem in the daylily scene has been, and continues to be, the huge number of 'look-alike' daylilies that are released each year at very high prices with little if anything to justify the price charged. There are too many new releases that do not justify their high price tag! There are too many hybridisers churning out minor variations on a theme or even releasing cultivars inferior to those already on the market. This is most unfortunate as it brings into question the ethics of those hybridisers who are beyond reproach and who have brought this flower to the standard of excellence it currently enjoys.

How do you advise people on how much to pay for a daylily? The only advice I can give is 'let the buyer beware'. Price should reflect quality but unfortunately, at times, it doesn't. The best advice is to purchase from a reputable nursery, preferably a specialist nursery. Reputable nurseries will have realistic market prices. Prices of the more expensive varieties will inevitably come down in time as supply and demand even out. If a cultivar is highly priced and there is buyer resistance the nursery will quickly find it has excess stock and the price will fall. Even when there are plenty of purchasers some cultivars multiply quickly and prices still fall. A highly priced cultivar that retains its high price does so usually for one of two reasons—it is in continuing high demand or it is a slow increaser. Often it is a combination of these two factors.

A further warning: a lower price for a particular variety from one nursery compared to another nursery may not reflect good value. The first responsibility of a reputable nursery is to provide a healthy, quality plant. A large double division of a daylily priced at $10 is far better value than a single division plant priced at $6 or more. Daylily price comparison can be difficult as the customer needs to know what they get for what they pay.

Most customers buy their quality daylilies from specialist nurseries and most specialist nurseries send out a double division (or more) plant or specify that their price is for a single fan. As the majority of sales by specialist nurseries are by mail order it is only by trial (hopefully not trial and error) or by recommendation that customers will feel comfortable with their supplier. In the 1990s there has been an explosion of smaller hobby nurseries throughout the world. Many are quite good, but some are of a dubious nature. It is for the customer to discover and deal with a supplier with whom they feel comfortable.

Another major factor in purchasing daylilies is the issue of 'extras'. Some nurseries provide generous bonus plants with any order and these 'surprises' often out-perform the purchased plants. Some nurseries will even allow the customer to select their own 'surprises' when stock allows.

Plants of different varieties do not necessarily conform to a predetermined size—remember some cultivars make small plants and others make very large plants.

To ensure satisfaction try to see flowers in bloom at specialist nurseries or in the gardens of growers in your area. Failing this, rely on the advice of your specialist nursery or experienced growers.

In recent years, more and more general nurseries have been selling potted daylilies. The quality of the flower on these plants varies greatly. Try to see the plant in bloom. There are some outstanding cultivars available as growers buy supplies from specialist nurseries and then pot them for sale. Others have been less than professional by using colour photos of named quality cultivars to sell reject seedlings. These are the kinds of practices which should be stamped out and the nursery industry should be self-regulating for the protection of customers.

There is always the question of newer varieties versus older varieties, and I have been asked many times to make recommendations. Invariably my advice goes along these lines. The new varieties are, in general, superior to those that have preceded them. If you are happy to pay for the latest and greatest and feel comfortable with what you are spending then this is the way to go. However, there are many outstanding cultivars available at moderate prices and if you want good performers with a minimal outlay then there is a long list of these good performers. The choice is yours—you should expect to pay for what you get but you should also expect to get what you pay for!

Clubs and societies

There is no doubt that garden clubs and specialist societies give members wonderful opportunities to meet others with common interests. There is always the chance to give, to receive, to exchange the benefits of one's gardening experiences and in practical terms to exchange the plants one grows. Specialist societies such as the Hemerocallis Society in the country you live in provide the opportunity to meet with other daylily enthusiasts and to exchange plants and many excellent cultivars can be obtained this way.

Invariably societies have display days, open days and show days. These special days are usually open to members and non-members alike and provide an excellent venue for gardeners to purchase plants often at bargain prices. The quality and presentation of the plant is not always top class but the price is always right! This is the opportunity to start or to enlarge a collection of daylilies. As daylily shows are held at or about peak bloom they also give prospective growers an ideal opportunity to see, evaluate and compare the daylily blooms.

Of course specialist societies provide many other facilities for their members and for the modest annual fee they provide excellent value for enthusiasts.

8 Gardening and landscaping

As previously noted, daylilies are easy plants to use in the garden because of their toughness and adaptability. There are very few plants which can be used in so many varied positions. Best bloom will always be obtained in a sunny position with good drainage. Fertile soil and adequate maintenance will enhance performance but daylilies will survive and perform well in less-than-perfect conditions and with less-than-perfect care.

The use of daylilies in the landscape can be as varied as the imagination of the gardener and with the wide colour range available there are daylilies for any colour scheme. Another bonus is the long flowering period and re-bloom which combine to ensure that daylilies can be used with a large range of companion plants, either in harmony or in contrast.

Specimen planting

Most gardens are planned and developed well before any daylilies are considered and this 'after-thought' planting results in daylilies being used as specimen plants. This is a successful way to grow a single cultivar or a few cultivars as the daylily is most competitive in a mixed planting without being invasive. Choice of cultivar for specimen planting is a highly individual one and many enthusiasts start out with a few specimen plants only to face a daylily 'takeover' in years to come.

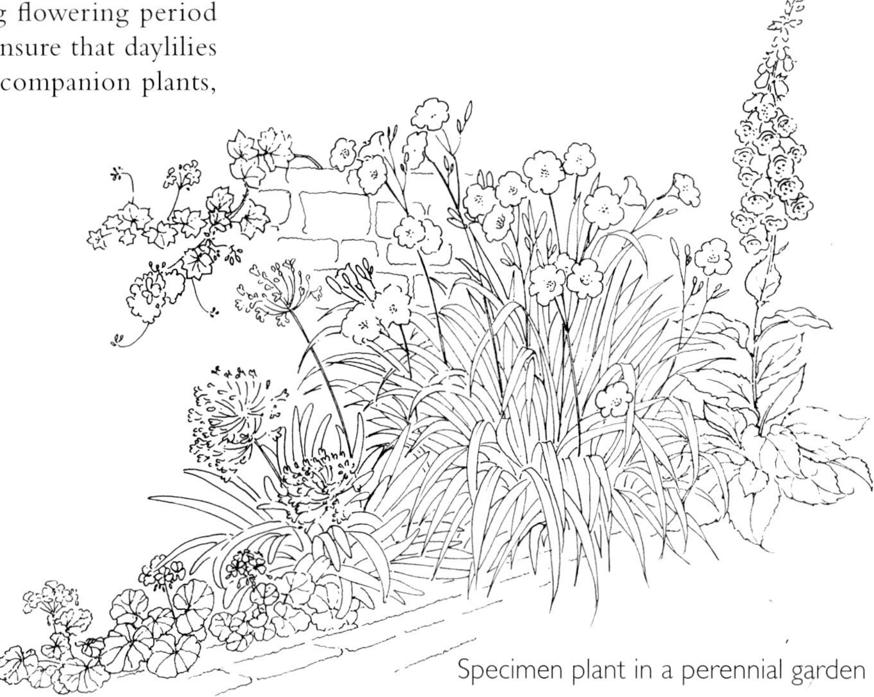

Specimen plant in a perennial garden

Opposite 'Dragon's Dreams'

Mass planting

Massed plantings of daylilies are spectacular. They can be planted in rows or drifts of the same or different cultivars. They can be used as a border for gardens or paths. They can be used in large banks and, as they are excellent soil retainers, they can be used very effectively to bind the soil and prevent erosion. This they do in a most colourful and practical way. An embankment covered in daylilies is a most spectacular blaze of colour for several months of the year and, even when not in flower, evergreen cultivars provide healthy, lush, attractive foliage.

When using daylilies in massed displays one has to be careful to consider growth habit. Using one cultivar is easy but when two or more cultivars are used, the plant habit is equally as important as the flower form and colour in providing harmony.

Because of their ease of cultivation and extended bloom period, daylilies are excellent plants for roadside plantings. I deplore the old cliché 'thrive on neglect' because they do not 'thrive' on neglect but they will certainly tolerate minimal care and still be very rewarding.

Daylilies are very useful for a driveway, an area of the garden which is important and can be difficult to maintain. Many a daylily has survived the minor 'accidents' associated with driveway planting. They are also tough enough to survive the exposure that a driveway inevitably experiences to the neighbourhood in general. Dogs, cats, the neighbour's children and the careless or inexperienced drivers of delivery vehicles can usually be handled with resilience. Be warned though—a daylily in full bloom is a spectacular sight and the one problem that cannot be ignored is the temptation they can create for some with itchy fingers. Daylilies occasionally can disappear from exposed positions at the hands of unwanted visitors.

Another major use of daylilies is around pools, on decks, patios or on terraces. What a wonderful plant the daylily is for poolside planting. Splashing from chlorinated or salt water presents no problem. Rough use from enthusiastic swimmers presents no long-term problem and the great bonus is the colour from extended bloom through most of the swimming season. For those with floodlit pools for night swimming the use of nocturnal daylilies, accented by spotlights or just generally lit, is ideal.

On a grander scale, daylilies are superb along the edges of lakes or ponds where they can be used as a dominant planting or to give accent in spot plantings. Whether they are used around pools or around lakes and ponds daylilies will achieve a lovely effect if planted so that the flowers are reflected in the water.

Daylilies are excellent in massed bedding around a single focus such as a tree, a statue, a sundial, a birdbath, or larger garden structures such as gazebos or rotundas. They can be planted in circles, squares or rectangles, they can be lined out or planted irregularly. You can plant one cultivar only or several different cultivars. I believe very strongly that gardeners should plant as they please in the garden, not as they feel others would

Daylilies used as a border edging

Daylily used for focus planting

like them to plant. Design and the use of plants are very personal. By all means make use of the expertise of professionals but always have that little bit of control to ensure you get what you want. Again I must stress that professional landscapers are trained and experienced in ensuring a pleasing final effect and their advice will always be valuable. If you are choosing your plants for a massed effect, always take care in considering the growth, height of scape and general plant habit as well as the more obvious factors of bloom colour and pattern.

The cottage garden

The use of perennials both as borders and in the traditional 'cottage garden' is very fashionable and the daylily has a significant place in each of these types of garden design. Much of the planting in these gardens is done with colour themes in mind and because of the huge range of colours available the daylily is an obvious choice for massed or spot planting.

Climatic conditions will determine the most suitable plants for perennial borders and cottage gardens but daylilies can be grown in any climatic conditions as long as suitable cultivars are chosen. Because of their ease of culture daylilies will be suitable companion plants for most, if not all, perennials and as they are not invasive they can be kept readily in check. I can think of no other perennial that is so adaptable and hence so suitable for a permanent position in the garden or so equally suitable to be moved around at the gardener's whim.

Daylily plant near a pond

Massed daylilies at Rainbow Ridge

Commercial plantings

Daylilies are very suitable for large commercial plantings such as in parks or public gardens. They are ideal for gardens associated with factories, shopping centres, schools and universities. They lend themselves to large plantings of massed colour which will be produced over many months. Many daylily flowers will fall gracefully once their one day of glory is over but for those where the spent flowers linger, the only major maintenance is to remove the spent flowers and to tidy up foliage from time to time.

Daylilies used near a pool

Opposite 'Elfin Escapade'

Potted colour

Daylilies are very suitable plants for pot culture and plants grown in containers can be used very effectively on account of the length and continuity of bloom and the fact that the container may be moved into a variety of suitable positions during the growing season.

As the typical daylily plant makes a thick mat of roots quite quickly they are best planted in large containers or tubs. In my experience, single or double divisions planted in 20 cm (8 in) pots will grow nicely and flower well in their first year. Even the weaker growers will become pot-bound after one season and although bloom will be good in the second season they would then have to be potted on. Because of their robust nature I would not recommend that standard large-flowered daylilies be grown in anything smaller than a 17.5 cm (7 in) pot. Some miniature and small-flowered daylilies can be grown on for sale in smaller containers but really only look their best when potted up to a 17.5 cm (7 in) or larger sized pot. I would suggest that the home gardener should be looking at a minimum 30 cm (12 in) tub for effective and continuous container cultivation.

Containers used should be reasonably deep to allow an adequate root run, should be well drained and should be filled to about 3–4 cm (about 1½ in) from the top with a well-composted soil or potting mix. Slight acidity (pH around 6.5) is preferred but not essential. A 1:1:1 mix of quality soil, peat moss and well-rotted compost or manure is an excellent medium. Ensure that adequate space is left at the top of the pot to facilitate watering and mulching. A teaspoon of 8–9 month slow release fertiliser is adequate and, if desired, the sprinkling of a weed germination inhibitor such as Ronstar or Rout will keep the pot clean of most weeds for 10–12 weeks. When using weed inhibitors take care to follow instructions and avoid spillage onto the foliage as it will mark and disfigure any foliage with which it comes in contact.

Plants suitable for use in containers would vary according to taste but I would favour the low-growing cultivars and would not consider using the very tall cultivars. As already stated, most miniature daylilies are excellent in containers. Three particularly beautiful larger flowered cultivars for pot culture are:

'Scarlet Orbit'—brilliant red;
'Lauren Leah'—cream;
'Ruffled Shawl'—pink.

Daylily in a container

Potted daylilies on a patio

Companion plants

What constitutes a 'companion plant'? I would suppose that companion plants, by definition, are plants that:

- can be grown together;
- look good together; and
- complement one another in the garden in growth and bloom.

I would further suppose that daylilies would only be considered as companion plants for other species and vice versa if the gardener finds them mutually attractive. All of this leads to the one basic question—what other plants can be grown with daylilies? The answer is a very broad 'anything that is suitable for the climate'.

Many perennials will not perform to satisfaction if planted in close proximity to trees but once again daylilies prove their versatility by being able to be grown right up to the canopy of large trees. It is undesirable to plant daylilies beneath the canopy as they will be too shaded to perform well and there is the added complication of possibly too much root competition. Daylilies will, however, grow and bloom in semi-shade and will compete with tree roots as long as they are given sufficient nutrient and water.

I have a personal affection for conifers of all sizes and a conifer and daylily garden has great appeal. The shape and texture of foliage of conifers is very desirable and they combine beautifully with daylilies. Most conifers are very attractive in the winter months when daylily bloom is at its lowest while the spectacular colour of summer bloom on the daylilies is accentuated by the conifer foliage.

Shrubs of all types are ideal for use as backdrops or for interspersing with daylilies. Their combined use is limited only by the imagination.

When used with other perennials, daylilies are superb. They are equally good when used with summer flowering annuals. There is an ease of design and culture when planting daylilies with annuals as the display is only to be maintained for one season. Many gardeners like to plant their daylilies very well spaced to allow for an updated annual display each year and this is a very desirable practice. Obviously, a great deal more care needs to be taken with mixed perennial planting as the current and future seasons have to be considered simultaneously. Fortunately, daylilies can be moved very easily and at most times of the year. They are undemanding and easy to re-establish.

Bulbs, corms and rhizomes are also suitable companions for daylilies but, from a personal

Daylilies at Rainbow Ridge

'Picadilly Princess' with vireya rhododendron 'Tropic Fanfare' in the background. *Photograph by Scott Alexander*

'Tiny Trumpeter'

Opposite 'Fairy Filigree'

viewpoint, are the least desirable because of the difficulty in keeping track of them and the added difficulty of maintaining those left in the ground. As the daylily grows and spreads it will inevitably cause problems with maintenance of bulbs, corms and rhizomes. Coupled with the maintenance problem is the fact that many bulbs, corms and rhizomes will not flower simultaneously with daylilies. In particular, those that flower in spring are usually looking less than attractive in early summer as the flowers are finished, the foliage is in decline and the daylilies are coming up to their best. The summer-flowering *Iris ensata* (Japanese iris) is a notable exception as it blooms simultaneously with the early daylilies but has a much shorter bloom period. *Iris ensata* will grow in similar conditions to daylilies but can in no way match their vigour. If left more than a couple of seasons closely planted *Iris ensata* will be over-run by the more vigorous daylilies. Care and planning are the secrets of success.

Roses are the most popular of all flowers and, for the beauty of the flowers, deservedly so. The successful use of roses and hemerocallis can create a stunning garden picture and, from personal experience, I can testify to the joys of using them together. Ten years ago the use of roses and daylilies would have had my unqualified endorsement. Now, there is still endorsement but it is certainly qualified. Roses are beautiful and easy to grow but not easy to grow well. Daylilies are beautiful and easy to grow! Both are susceptible to attack from mites. These minute insects can cause severe damage to the foliage of both daylilies and roses; when they are grown together daylilies can cause problems for roses and vice versa if the climate and weather conditions are conducive to attack by spider mites. In areas free from these pests I strongly recommend the use of roses and daylilies as companion plants. In areas where spider mites are a problem the mites can be controlled, but with increasing difficulty, by the use of insecticides. Alternatively, and this is my preference, spider mites can be kept under control by the use of predatory mites which do not attack the foliage of roses or daylilies but do attack the mites which do attack the foliage.

One other piece of advice on the use of roses and daylilies is to plant and maintain the daylilies sufficiently away from the roses so that a free flow of air is maintained around the rose plants. This helps considerably in the prevention of fungus diseases of the rose foliage. Daylily plants are virtually non-susceptible to fungus diseases.

I have considered giving a long list of recommended trees, shrubs, perennials, annuals, bulbs, corms and rhizomes, conifers and roses but, in reality, all I would be doing is giving a long list of my personal favourites, many of which would be unsuitable for the reader's climatic conditions. Why be specific when one can speak generally and leave the specifics to the taste of the individual? If you wish to use daylilies in a small or large planting with or without accompanying plants DO IT. The choice is yours. You will never regret it!

9
Pests and diseases

Pests

If there are pests in the garden, then daylilies will, at least to some extent, be affected. There are pests in every garden but some gardens are better maintained than others. Daylilies have been known traditionally to be pest-free but this, alas, is not completely true. Let me hasten to add, however, that daylilies are easy-care plants, in fact, *the* lazy gardener's plants that are not unduly affected by pests or diseases. There is no plant that I know that gives as much reward for as little effort.

Aphids can be a problem, particularly in spring and autumn. They will often hide and multiply rapidly in the foliage at the base of the fans near the crown. They feed on the tips of the new emerging foliage and often on the young buds, causing foliage to arch over, be malformed and unattractive and leaving buds malformed and even discoloured. Aphids will transmit diseases and are responsible for the transmission of virus infection but viruses in daylilies are very rare.

Aphids can be controlled in a variety of ways and the simplest of all is to just hose them off the plants. They can also be washed off with soapy water or sprayed with insecticides. I prefer not to use insecticides, if at all possible, but when necessary I have found that Folimat is excellent in the control of aphids. This is a systemic insecticide spray which gets into the system of the plant and will provide protection for three to four weeks after application. It has the added advantages of no noticeable odour and helps in the control of spider mites to some degree.

Spider mites are the worst pests that daylilies encounter and they can absolutely ravage daylily plants before the gardener is aware of their presence. These minute insects are not readily observed by the naked eye but they infect the lower leaves, eating the chlorophyll and leaving a trail of devastation as they work up the plant. Leaves are left debilitated and unsightly as they brown off and die. Red spider, as the most common of these mites is known, is particularly active and increases rapidly in hot dry weather. It does not affect the flower but the foliage can be made so unattractive when badly affected that the overall effect is not pleasant. Let me stress that these mites are not active every season and in many climates are of little or no concern. Let me also stress that, if they are active, they can be a major problem.

One has no control over the weather and hot dry spells can occur in most climates. As the mites do not like moisture it is advisable to keep plants well watered when the weather is dry. As this is also a good cultural practice it is logical that most good gardeners will do their best to prevent mite problems.

Control of spider mites is not easy. Chemical sprays can often cause as many problems as they cure. Kelthane has been a generally recommended insecticide for spider mites but it is dangerous to daylily plants and should not be used. The warning bears repetition—*under no circumstances* should Kelthane be used on daylilies. Plictran is a safer and more effective controller of red spider and for minor infestations will give good control.

'Siloam Dream Baby' with 'Heart's Glee' (foreground)

Unfortunately those mites that do survive build up an immunity and once you have started the spraying process you become committed to stronger and stronger sprays. Simultaneously, the mites that survive become stronger and stronger, more immune and soon you have a 'super race' of spider mites with which to contend. The ultimate insecticide to use against mites is Temik (an aldicarb compound) which is highly poisonous if swallowed, inhaled or absorbed through the skin. I believe that Temik has been taken off the market in Australia and many other countries and, even if it is available, I would recommend its use only as a last resort. I can testify to its effectiveness against mites, but . . . what of its effect on humans?

In these days of environmental awareness there is a strong emphasis on natural control of pests and nowhere is this more evident than in the control of spider mites. It has been well known for many years that there is a 'super mite', much larger than the sap-sucking spider mites. This super mite does not feed on the foliage of plants as its smaller cousins do but is a fierce predator which feeds on other mites. When introduced into the garden these predatory mites will feed ravenously on the spider mites and will quickly reduce the population. This can be a problem in itself as the predatory mites can be left without food if the job is too well done. The other problems are that the predatory mites are expensive to purchase and that they are unable to survive the winter cold in all but the warmest of climates and so must be replaced each year. A further problem is that there is no point in introducing the predatory mites until there is a start to a spider mite problem. Gardeners find themselves reactive rather than proactive in the mite control situation and I, for one, do not like that. Let me hasten to add that I have used predatory mites for quite a few years now and, within the above stated limitations, I have found them very effective. We purchase ours from the University of Western Sydney and I am sure that enthusiasts will be able to locate a source of supply in their area. Care needs to be taken with the use of insecticides when using predatory mites as most insecticides will kill predatory mites. Plictran can be used with care. Advice should be sought from your supplier of predatory mites on which sprays can be used.

Thrips can also be a problem but to a much lesser degree than mites. These tiny insects do not attack the foliage but can damage newly opened buds. They enter into the bud and eat the tissue on the inside, damaging the flower and leaving white scars on the open blooms which become decidedly unattractive. Control is very difficult and once thrips are around, the use of pesticides will often magnify the problems, making flowers more unattractive than the thrips would do. A good watering program is definitely beneficial and daylilies will benefit from overhead watering if this can be done while the flowers are, in general, in bud, i.e. very early in the morning or alternatively very late in the day. Daylilies are one of the very few plants that do benefit from overhead watering.

It has fascinated me over the years to observe the way certain daylilies are affected by thrip while others are left completely alone. A particular variety that comes to mind is 'Elles', one of the most beautiful of pink daylilies but an absolute martyr to thrip.

If one must resort to chemical control I would once again recommend Folimat. This will give good control of thrip, excellent control of aphids and some control of red spider with a minimum of undesirable effects. I believe it is currently the best pesticide available for all around protection of daylilies.

Slugs and snails love to live in the moist protective foliage of daylilies and they can become a problem if allowed to thrive. They are at their worst in early spring when plants are making their initial growth and they can also become a problem as the daylilies come into bloom in late spring to early summer. I have only seen slugs and snails climb the flowering scapes on limited occasions but when they do they can really make a mess of beautiful flowers. It is in the interests of the gardener to eliminate or at least limit their activity early in the growing season.

Protection from snails and slugs can take a variety of forms. Perhaps the simplest is the search and destroy method. Snails and slugs are most active after dark and they can readily be dispatched when found. For the squeamish, a pinch of salt is very effective as a killer. Of course this leaves all the ones not found to enjoy life to the full. A more certain approach is to use pelleted or powdered snail baits. These are effective but must be replenished at regular intervals, particularly after watering or natural rainfall. Care must also be taken to ensure that household pets are kept away from the snail baits. Placing pellets or powder in a bottle ensures that birds are not unwitting victims.

Our best results for snail and slug elimination have been with the use of Mesurol, a powder which is mixed with water and sprayed on the foliage. Sufficient should be used to cover the foliage and dribble down onto the crown. It is expensive to purchase but very effective and an initial spray at the start of the growing season with a follow-up as the flower scapes form gives excellent protection. The spray should be administered late in the afternoon and both watering and rain should be avoided for two nights to ensure success. If you get heavy rain after spraying a follow-up spray may be necessary.

Nematodes are tiny worms found in soils and they can be a problem on rare occasions. They will attack the roots of plants but I have not observed them as a noticeable problem with daylilies. A 'one-off' spraying of the soil with Nemacur will give effective control of nematodes.

There can always be problems of a minor nature with other biting, sucking or chewing insects but, in general, they leave daylilies alone and any problem is fleeting and relatively minor.

Birds will sometimes take a fancy to the daylily flowers but again the problems are insignificant. Even our notorious white cockatoos have only inflicted very minor damage over the years.

I have also read of daylilies being attacked by a tiny insect called gall fly but I have had no experience with this pest.

Diseases

Daylilies are among the healthiest plants in commerce. There is little doubt that the chemical companies which supply sprays and poisons would be long out of business if all plants were as resistant to disease as daylilies.

Three diseases that are mentioned in relation to daylilies are crown rot, 'spring sickness', and leaf spot (or leaf streak). In over 30 years of growing these plants I have not experienced crown rot or 'spring sickness' in my garden so I must write from the accounts of others.

Crown rot can be experienced in wet, humid conditions, particularly if plants are in poorly drained soil. It can take the form of a bacterial soft rot as experienced in bearded iris or a fungal rot. This is a problem experienced mainly in tropical areas. The best treatment is to dig the plant, remove the infected parts and allow the plant to dry out before replanting. A precautionary spray or soaking in an antibiotic such as aureomycin or streptomycin can be helpful. In general, if the plant has been left so that the crown has commenced to rot it will be lost.

Spring sickness is a problem which has not been observed in Sydney's temperate climate but it has been reported in areas where there are heavy frosts and snow. The foliage will turn brown and then rot. If allowed to progress too far the plant will be lost and the only treatment is to lift the plant, remove the affected part, keep the plant dry and hope!

Leaf spot (leaf streak) is a fungal disease which manifests itself as brown spots and markings on the outer foliage and also as pale, near-white streaks in the foliage. It is unsightly rather than dangerous, is not often seen and can be controlled by preventative spraying with Mancozeb. Once the plant is infected the foliage will not be 'cured' so infected foliage should be removed and burned and a preventative spray used to keep the new foliage clean.

10
Photographing daylilies

For many growers it is a natural extension of their interest and hobby to wish to record their daylilies on film. It is very important to realise the limitations of any equipment you have and to attempt to take only those photographs that have a reasonable chance of success. Ideally, a single lens reflex camera with a macro lens will enable you to capture most, if not all, of the daylily photographs you desire. It is axiomatic that the better the equipment, the better the potential of the photo taken but no matter how high the quality of the equipment much depends on the art and skill of the photographer.

Photographing daylilies is a fascinating experience as the flower can vary so much in the single day of life both in terms of colour and form, and flowers can vary considerably from day to day. Such is the variation that one could obtain a collection of photographs of any one particular daylily and, in fact, this is exactly what I have done. There is no specific time of day best suited for daylily photography but flowers do not reach their peak until mid to late morning on a typical summer day. Remember also that many daylilies, particularly the darker coloured cultivars, will be past their best by mid afternoon in hot conditions.

Daylily photographs can be taken as portraits of single blooms, scapes carrying a number of single blooms, clumps with many blooms in evidence or general landscaping photographs.

Opposite 'Tiny Talisman'

Beautiful results will be obtained for single bloom photography by looking straight into the flower while interesting variations can be obtained by photographing the flower at various angles. When taking photographs of daylilies in full sun one has to be careful to avoid shadows cast on the flower to give an uneven effect. This can be achieved in two ways—by using a reflector or by using a diffuser. A simple reflector can be made by using any shiny surface to reflect light back into the flower and 'fill in' any uneven lighting gaps. I use foil spread over a solid base.

Even better results can be obtained by using a diffusing medium such as perspex to spread the direct light from the sun more evenly.

Either way the quality of photographs will be greatly improved on any attempts to use direct sunlight. Of course, some very interesting effects can be obtained by the varied use of lighting.

In any 'portrait' flower photography, it is essential to have a wide depth of field to allow the outer edges of petals, the throat or heart of the flower, and the sexual parts, all of which are in different planes, to all be in focus together. Once again, very interesting results can be obtained by deliberately throwing part of the photo out of focus. To keep all of the flower in focus the photographer needs to use fast film—I suggest 100 ASA or more—and to have an aperture selection of f8, f11 or f16. In obtaining this clarity the shutter speed will often have to be slow, with speeds as low as 1/30 sec or even slower, and so it is recommended that a tripod be used to keep the camera steady. It is pointless to go to all the trouble of ensuring accurate focus only to achieve a blurred image because of camera shake.

Daylily scapes are often not easy to photograph as the open flowers are invariably facing in different directions. The more open flowers the better the scape but the more difficult it becomes to photograph. This problem can be overcome to a certain extent by twisting the flowers and thereby re-positioning them to obtain the optimum effect. It is essential that the scape be groomed to get the best results. All dead flowers should be removed and care should be taken to ensure that the foliage is clean and the background is attractive or suitably thrown out of focus by selecting an aperture in the f4 or f5.6 range. It is usually beneficial to take several photographs of the same scape with a full range of f stops.

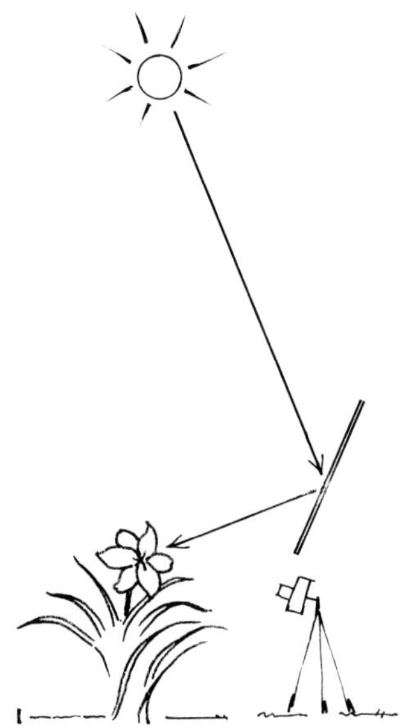

Photographing a daylily using a reflector

To obtain a satisfactory photograph of a daylily clump it is essential to groom the whole clump with particular attention to spent flowers and clean foliage. Flowers that were open on the previous day are the worst offenders as they can look quite messy while earlier blooms will often self groom. Care needs to be taken to remove any completely spent spikes as they will look most unsightly in a photograph. Often clumps have unfilled gaps which will ruin the composition of the photograph. These gaps can be filled by repositioning scapes from elsewhere and filling in to provide an attractively composed photograph.

Landscape photographs require less critical attention to individual grooming and more critical attention to composition. It is so easy to allow unwanted material to creep into the photograph and spoil the overall effect.

With all this advice on grooming and composition there is the final issue of the 'law of diminishing returns'. Much depends on what you as photographer want. For many, a simple record of a beautiful subject is all they require and to spend a lot of time in preparation is time wasted. Remember, however, that it is far better to take all the recommended care and to be pleased with your results than to take many more photographs and find none of them satisfactory.

FAST is an appropriate word to remember for the inexperienced photographer. Quite often if you go FAST you will be unhappy with your results but FAST can be used as a key word:

F = Focus;
A = Aperture;
S = Speed;
T = Think.

Focus—Ensure that you have a clear, sharp subject with an appealing background. Pleasing backgrounds can be either in or out of focus. Remember that f stops

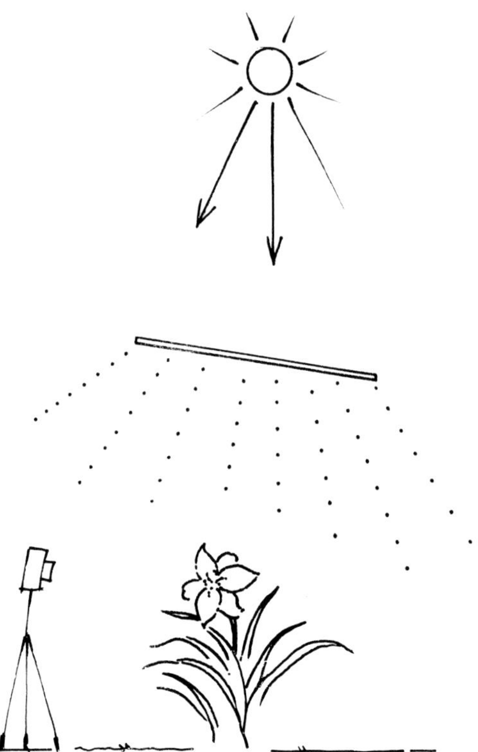

Photographing a daylily using a diffuser

with high numbers i.e. f11, f16 will have more of your subject in focus than f stops with low numbers i.e. f2.8, f4. Remember also that the use of a tripod will assist in keeping your camera steady and should eliminate blurred images through camera shake.

Aperture—Try to work at f8, f11, f16 or more to obtain a lot of image clear in the finished product. Remember that you can obtain some lovely special effects by varying your aperture. Use a reflector or diffuser to obtain even lighting but remember that allowance must be made for the light used. A good light meter is essential and most quality cameras do have good in-built light meters these days.

Speed—Try to work at 1/60 second or faster, preferably 1/125 or 1/250 second. Otherwise use a tripod. The use of faster film (rated 100 ASA or more) will allow you to use faster speeds with the same aperture.

Think—Try to think primarily about what you are attempting to achieve. Most thought should be given to the composition of the photograph and such facets as framing the subject, the foreground, the background, the grooming of the daylilies and the positioning of the camera are all important.

In writing this chapter I have refrained from giving advice as the whether you should photograph your daylilies on positive film or transparencies or on negative film for the production of colour prints. Modern advances in printing are such that printing from transparencies is of a high standard so you can have the best of both worlds. Similar advances in movie photography have now enabled inexperienced photographers to record their precious daylilies on video. This has the added advantage of instant replay and immediate response to the result. I have also refrained from giving advice on the many brands and types of film available. Advice of this type would be more suitable for a book on photography.

In conclusion I must reiterate that the daylily is a beautiful flower that lends itself admirably to the photographer's art. Daylily photographs are comparable to or better than those I have seen of any floral subjects.

11
Hybridising

There is a degree of creativity in all of us and I am sure that many gardeners have, at some time, thought it would be nice to develop a flower that was their very own. Daylily enthusiasts have a wonderful opportunity to do just that as the daylily ranks among the easiest of plants for hybridisers to cross-pollinate, set seed, raise the seed and see the results of their work—all in a very short two-year period from doing the cross to viewing the resultant flower.

Hybridisers can be classified into three general categories:

- those who observe seed set naturally, collect it and plant it with high hopes but little aspiration;
- those who happily dab a little pollen around from one flower to another, again with high hopes but little planning or expectation; and
- those who are serious hybridisers, varying in intensity, but with some kind of scientific approach. There is little doubt that the 'scientific' hybridiser will have the greatest chance of success.

The scientific hybridiser may work at the very basic level of thinking that two flowers may go well together and hence a cross is made. At a more developed level the hybridiser will observe the plants, read and study family trees, form hypotheses about the results of using certain parents, set aims and then plan crosses to achieve these aims. When it is decided to perform the cross a large number of crosses should be performed to raise as many seedlings as possible and thereby explore the full potential of the cross. Many pods may need to be set to test any hypothesis fully. It is also advisable to reverse pod and pollen parents. Many daylilies are reluctant to set pods, others will not produce viable pollen. Some are both pod and pollen fertile, others are completely infertile. It must be noted that it is considerably easier to set pods from diploid crosses than from tetraploid crosses and that a diploid pod may contain up to 40 or more seeds while a tetraploid pod will contain considerably fewer seeds, often only four or five or even fewer than that. Remember also that diploid cultivars should only be crossed with diploid cultivars and that tetraploids should only be crossed with other tetraploids.

Opposite 'Patchwork Puzzle'

Then there are the philosophical issues to be considered. What are you trying to do? Hemerocallis hybridisers are primarily concerned with form and colour. The main aim is to produce a different and hopefully a better flower. This can be broken down into various facets—such as the shape of the flower, the size of the flower, its colour, the colour pattern. There are other facets such as substance, bloom timing, bloom period, sun-fastness and so the list goes on. Remember that, if you perceive that a flower has a fault or a failing, crossing it with another flower with the same problem will only reinforce the defect. Parents should be selected to eliminate problems, not to reinforce them.

Before performing crosses it would be beneficial to have some knowledge of the potential of the selected parents. This is where specialist societies are of great benefit to their members. Membership of a daylily society gives the enthusiast access by both word of mouth and written communication to the experiences of others and much time and effort can be saved by learning from the experiences, both positive and negative, of those who have had hybridising experience.

While the main point of most hybridising efforts has been and will continue to be the improvement of and variation in the flower there are other equally important aspects of the plant. Of prime importance is the plant itself, its growth, vigour, health, flower production and general performance. Of equal importance is the scape on which the flowers are produced and such things as bud count, flowering habit, branching, spacing and repeat bloom are all of significance. I lament the fact that many modern hybridisers have lost sight of the big picture. Their efforts are concentrated on producing pretty flowers and other important aspects are being overlooked. I do not question the overall importance of the flower but stress that all aspects of the plant should be considered.

Once all these ideas have been digested and a logical aim devised and parents selected, there are the mechanics of the cross-pollination to be worked out. Timing is significant as results in terms of pods successfully set can be significantly raised if the crosses are made when flowers are most receptive. Early morning is the best time to start—most serious hybridisers will have all their day's work completed between 10 a.m. and 11 a.m. Pollen should be dry and the female parent flower should also be dry so that wet days, days with early morning dews and overhead watering prior to crossing should be avoided. From my experience a significantly larger number of 'takes' will be observed if the pod (female) parent is not in direct sunlight. Shades and covers of various types can be used to assist pollination. More crosses will 'take' if pollination is done on cool days.

The actual doing of the cross is easy. An anther from the selected pollen parent is collected—tweezers will help but it can be done by hand—and the pollen is then brushed across the stigmatic lip of the pod parent.

Other than ensuring that the stigmatic lip is not unduly wet there are no special requirements for the flower onto which the cross is to be made. Some hybridisers will remove all the anthers from the female parent. There is no doubt that this helps to ensure there is no self-fertilisation but to me, it is an unnecessary chore. Selecting suitable pollen can be more difficult, particularly if the garden is alive with pollen-loving insects. Ideally, you want fresh and plentiful pollen and this can often be obtained early in the day by opening the buds that are about to bloom. Reject any hardened crusty pollen and then store the ripe pollen ready for the morning's work. Any unused pollen can be stored in the crisper compartment of a refrigerator. Pollen to be stored over a longer period should be kept in containers with some silica gel to keep the pollen firm. If the pollen becomes too moist it is rarely viable.

Once the cross has been made the female parent flower should be labelled and the cross recorded. Keeping accurate records is very important for any serious hybridiser. It is only by keeping records that one can learn about the hybridising potential of the plants being used.

Pollinating a daylily

Covered pod

In recording a cross the pod parent is always written first. Thus if the pollen from 'Vintage Bordeaux' is taken and put onto a flower of 'Scarlet Orbit' the cross is recorded as 'Scarlet Orbit' x 'Vintage Bordeaux'. As well as recording the cross that is made and attaching a label around the base of the pollinated flower it is a valuable exercise to keep separate written records. Such things as the crosses made, the date, the time of day, the successes/failures and all other relevant information will build up into an invaluable source of accumulated knowledge. Written records are of value if tags on flowers are lost or destroyed. It is desirable to read, to listen and to learn about hybridising from the experiences of others but by far the best teacher is personal experience. You will learn what is and what is not effective and you will learn what information is of value and what is not. A written record of your experiences is a ready source of information for future projects.

When you have completed the cross and made any records that you wish it is not the end of the adventure, only the beginning. Within three to four days you will notice a swelling of the ovary at the base of the pollinated flower if your pollination has been successful. Unfertilised flowers will wither and usually fall off the scape in that same period. A fertilised ovary will take from 60–80 days to produce mature seeds ready for collection. In that period the developing seed pod needs to be protected from predators. Immediate covering with an old stocking or a commercial crop cover such as 'Evolution Cloth' will ensure protection from the various eating or chewing predators without, in any way, spoiling the ripening process.

Covering a pod also has the added benefit of retaining the seed should the seed pod open prior to collection. As they approach maturity the pods turn from a green colouration to brown, begin to dry and start to crack open at the top. At this stage they should be checked daily and harvested before the seed pod cracks open.

Once harvested, the seed pods should be stored until ready for planting. It is of little importance what form the containers for storage take—use whatever suits you best. I have, at different stages, used paper envelopes, old slide film containers, plastic take-away food containers and glass jars.

Planting time will differ according to climate and it is best to learn from your own experience. In hot tropical climates seed can be planted immediately while in cold areas it may be kept stored until the following spring. Experiment to discover your own preferred time. Some hybridisers soak the seed for 24 hours before planting while others insert a small nick in the outer casing of the seed before sowing. It is claimed that these practices increase both the speed and quantity of germination.

Seeds are usually sown into a seed-raising mix in pots, cold frames or directly into the garden. Again, you will discover your preferred option. Germination can be erratic and it will depend on your timing and your climate as to whether you see your precious seedlings in just a few days or have to wait several weeks. Experience will quickly establish what is best for you. Raising the seedlings is not difficult and the rate of growth will depend on initial sowing conditions. Pot sown seedlings can usually be set out in garden rows within two months of germination.

Many hybridisers commence their campaigns by using only those flowers which are out at a given time. As they advance to the pre-planned cross stage pollen has to be collected and stored as mentioned previously. Once collected the pollen should be scraped into an empty gelatin capsule, labelled and placed in a small plastic container into which has been placed some silica gel and the whole lot kept in a refrigerator. When ready for use, remove the pollen, allow it to warm to room temperature and then proceed with the cross.

Once involved in a hybridising campaign it is very desirable to have goals and to work towards these goals. In evaluating your own seedlings you need to be ruthless and retain only those which are distinctively different from cultivars already named or obvious improvements on existing named cultivars. When it comes to a question of naming and registering a seedling or not, the best advice is to be guided by your instincts and also to seek the opinion of a knowledgeable associate who will give an honest evaluation. Remember also that cultivars will not always perform well everywhere and it is often a good idea to have seedlings spread around to knowledgeable growers for their evaluation before these seedlings are named and registered.

The worldwide registration of new daylilies is done through the American Hemerocallis Society but other countries with specialist hemerocallis societies can assist you, for example, the Daylily Society in Australia has a registrar who will assist with the naming and registering of new cultivars.

12
Daylilies for eating

A major problem for any hybridiser of plants is the disposal of unwanted seedlings—not so with daylily hybridisers; if you don't want them in the garden for floral display you can eat them!

Daylilies have been used for centuries by the Chinese in their cooking and the daylily is an ideal vegetable in that all its parts are edible. Daylilies are high in protein, high in Vitamin A and Vitamin C and low in fat. They are also rich in minerals.

Daylily stalks can be cut just above the crown and the tender inner section can be boiled for a few minutes and eaten just as asparagus with butter. These stalks can also be sliced and added to salads.

The small 'tubers' attached to the roots and having the appearance of mini potatoes are also usable. The older soft tubers should be discarded and the young, firm and crisp tubers can be enjoyed raw for a sweet nutty flavour or can be used in salads, boiled or creamed. These young 'tubers' are white, distinct from the older brown ones and their taste has been described as resembling that of peas, nuts, radish or water chestnut. Their taste has also been described as 'bean-like', 'mushroom-like' and 'asparagus-like'. To discover how you would evaluate their taste the best suggestion I can make is to try them yourself.

The daylily flower can be collected for eating at any stage of blooming. It is generally accepted that the buds are at their best for eating when they are full so they are picked on the day before opening. They are an excellent substitute for green beans if boiled for four minutes and served with butter and salt. They can also be dipped in thick egg batter and fried in hot oil. The open flower can be treated in exactly the same way and there are those aesthetic gourmets who want the best of both worlds and so enjoy the beauty of the flower and then use the spent blooms for cooking with no less desirable results.

The flavour of soups and stews is enhanced by using buds or flowers which should be added during the last minutes that the dishes are simmered. If there is an excess of flowers for summer use, when stews and soups are not so popular in this country, they can be stored away. The blooms can be dried in a warm room, stored in glass jars and used in the winter months when these foods are popular. They can also be deep frozen for later use. They should be blanched for three to four minutes, placed in cold water and then frozen. Daylilies freeze as well as any other standard garden vegetable and may be enjoyed throughout the year. The buds and spent blooms are usually frozen because of ease of handling.

Daylilies of almost any colour can be used but it is said that red ones have a bitter taste. To be safe use the yellows, oranges and pastels. The darker flowered cultivars may be an acquired taste.

When daylily buds are dropped into hot water they have a tendency to open so, if you wish the buds to remain closed pick them about two days before their normal time to open. To freeze, bring blanching kettle to a rolling boil and drop in enough daylilies to be covered. After the water returns to a boil, blanch for three minutes. Remove and chill in cold water, drain well and pack in freezer bags.

Opposite 'Butterfly Charm'

Daylilies are nutritious but have medicinal value as well. They have been used extensively by the Chinese both as painkillers and as treatment for various diseases so it would seem that they are not only an attractive and tasty vegetable but a valuable health food as well.

Fried daylilies

(non-scented cultivars preferred)

Dip approximately one dozen fresh or thawed daylilies in beaten egg (one egg is sufficient to coat one dozen daylilies). Roll in a mixture of flour, salt and onion powder. Sauté in hot oil until crisp.

Sautéed daylily

Put thawed or fresh daylilies in a non-stick skillet or shallow pan, salt, cover with water and let simmer until tender. Do not overcook but be sure all moisture is used up. Remove from pan, add butter if desired, sprinkle well with onion powder and serve while hot.

Daylily bud casserole

10 cups daylily buds
3-4 strips of bacon
2 onions, sliced
1 can sliced mushrooms
1 can cream of mushroom soup
1 can water chestnuts

Cook bacon until crisp. Remove from pan, crumble, and set aside. Brown onions slowly in bacon drippings. Add ½ to ¾ cup of water. Bring to boil and add daylily buds. Season with salt and pepper to taste. Cook until tender, being careful not to overcook. Add drained mushrooms and water chestnuts, sliced or whole. Slowly and gently fold in undiluted soup. Turn into a casserole dish, garnish top with crumbled bacon and bake in 180°C (350°F) oven until crumbly.

Daylily soup

500 g (16 oz) pork strips, cubed
5 cups water
1 cup potato, cubed
2 cups daylily buds
1 onion
2–3 pieces of ginger
salt, pepper to taste
sherry

Chop the onion and sear with the pork strips. Add a dessertspoon of sherry, bring to the boil and add the water. Add the potato cubes, salt and pepper to taste and then simmer gently for 30 minutes. Garnish with daylilies and ginger and then serve when hot.

Daylily chicken

2 fillets chicken breast
1 onion
3 cups daylily buds
1 teaspoon ground ginger
1 teaspoon soya sauce
1 teaspoon plain flour
3 teaspoons olive oil
salt, pepper to taste

Slice the chicken breast thinly and chop the onion finely. Mix the chicken, half the onion, pepper, soya sauce, flour and ginger. Fry quickly in the olive oil for 2 minutes. Remove the chicken from the pan and brown the remaining half of the onion in the oil. Add in the daylily buds, pour in ¼ cup of water and add salt. Simmer gently, return the chicken and allow the whole meal to heat before serving.

And so there it is!

The daylily is a plant which can enrich not only your garden but your table.

I can reflect on the many pleasures that daylilies have given me over so many years.
I remember the hybrids available some 30 years ago
and I am dazzled by the advances that have been made in form, colour and pattern.
To all gardeners and non-gardeners, I can only advise you to do yourself a favour …
grow these wonderful plants and add a new dimension to your life.

General index

Index of cultivars

Index of daylily cultivars

Photographs indicated by italic type

Q

R

S

T

U

V

W

Y

Z